CW01457774

Jesus as Divine Suicide

Jesus as Divine Suicide

The Death of the Messiah in Galatians

JOEL L. WATTS

PICKWICK *Publications* · Eugene, Oregon

JESUS AS DIVINE SUICIDE
The Death of the Messiah in Galatians

Copyright © 2019 Joel L. Watts. All rights reserved. Except for brief quotations in critical publications or reviews, no part of this book may be reproduced in any manner without prior written permission from the publisher. Write: Permissions, Wipf and Stock Publishers, 199 W. 8th Ave., Suite 3, Eugene, OR 97401.

Pickwick Publications
An Imprint of Wipf and Stock Publishers
199 W. 8th Ave., Suite 3
Eugene, OR 97401

www.wipfandstock.com

PAPERBACK ISBN: 978-1-5326-5716-0
HARDCOVER ISBN: 978-1-5326-5717-7
EBOOK ISBN: 978-1-5326-5718-4

Cataloguing-in-Publication data:

Names: Watts, Joel L., author.

Title: Jesus as divine suicide : the death of the Messiah in Galatians / Joel L. Watts.

Description: Eugene, OR: Pickwick Publications, 2019 | Includes bibliographical references.

Identifiers: ISBN 978-1-5326-5716-0 (paperback) | ISBN 978-1-5326-5717-7 (hardcover) | ISBN 978-1-5326-5718-4 (ebook)

Subjects: LCSH: Bible. Galatians—Criticism, interpretation, etc. | Bible. Galatians—Theology. | Jesus Christ—Crucifixion—Biblical teaching.

Classification: BS2685.55.G35 W15 2019 (paperback) | BS2685.55.G35 (ebook)

Manufactured in the U.S.A.   06/20/19

Quotations marked NETS are taken from *A New English Translation of the Septuagint,* © 2007 by the International Organization for Septuagint and Cognate Studies, INC. Used by permission of Oxford University Press. All rights reserved.

Scripture quotations taken from the Revised English Bible (REB), copyright © Oxford University Press and Cambridge University Press 1989. All rights reserved.

Omnipotentis Domini misericordiam depraecemur, ut acceptum re-
ferat divina dignatio quidquid altaribus suis infert humana sedulitas.
Ratas faciat praeces et vota cunctorum; et quod devotio inpendit ad
gratiam, poscentibus profeciat ad salutem.

—Ancient Gallic Missal

Contents

Preface | ix

CHAPTER 1
Introduction | 1

CHAPTER 2
The Social Science Contexts | 29

CHAPTER 3
Self-Inflicted Death among Jewish Sources | 53

CHAPTER 4
The Roman Devotio | 88

CHAPTER 5
Early Christian Views on Self–Inflicted Death | 120

CHAPTER 6
Reading Galatians in Light of the Devotio | 132

CHAPTER 7
Conclusion | 146

A Bibliography of Selected Works | 149

Preface

To tell someone Jesus committed suicide rarely leaves room for qualification before an emotional reaction is issued. Over the years of expressing this idea to colleagues in the academic field, I came across perplexed looks. Some in the mental health field refused to hear it. However, as I progressed in both, I found new ways of introducing the topic, beginning with the qualification first. This book, I hope, allows for the qualification to be met, our anachronism to be explored, and an argument to be made—even if all three are controversial. It is not my intent to be scandalous for scandal's sake; however, in using the word "suicide" I hope to carry the current emotional connections to the word into the past. I feel this is the only way to get past two millennia of theological speculation and into the minds of the first century writers recovering from the trauma of the death of Jesus.

This project began as a dissertation under Dr. François Tolmie at the University of the Free State; however, my career changed course when I entered the clinical mental health field. Since then, I have decided to focus on mental health, including suicidal and delusional clients, while attempting to keep at least part of a foot in the academic world. I have written some of this work with the latter career in mind attempting to keep a somber and reflective tone, especially knowing that someone reading this will have had a loved one attempt or complete the act of suicide, often with no explanation. As I write this, the Centers for Disease Control issued a report noting that with the dramatic increase of suicides in the United States, the American life expectancy has decreased. I cannot help but to include that mood in my current writing.

In attempting to reach a wider audience, I have limited quotes in original languages, unless necessary. Most are in familiar English translations, something I hope provides access to those wishing to investigate the death of Jesus as a divine suicide, regardless of academic training. I have curtailed some of the arguments, attempting to focus only several specific areas. I have also attempted to make the argument explorable.

I wish to think Leigh Anne, my wife who had to listen to this each step of the way; Dr. Chris Spinks, my editor at Pickwick; Dr. David Watson, Dr. Jim West, Dr. Daniel Rodriguez, Anthony Lawson, Scott Fritzsche, Evan Rohrs-Dodge—early non-judgmental readers; and Dr. Randy Flanagan who told me that a certain denomination does not require us to think a certain way, only to think. I am able to live out my faith and question it each step of the way due to that statement, even if I am no longer part of that denomination. I will always express my gratitude to Dr. Vivian Johnson, currently at United Theological Seminary, who taught me the value of the argument, to look for the merits in how someone argued, and to listen even if I ultimately disagree. My thanks as well to Rabbi Victor Urecki for giving answers to my questions and access to the library at B'nai Jacob Synagogue in Charleston, West Virginia during the early days of this project. To my friend from across time, Marcus Annaeus Lucanus, who gave us our Cato. Finally, to my Lord and my Savior, Jesus Christ, for the peace you earned for me.

Joel L. Watts
Delta, Colorado
Advent, 2018

Chapter 1

Introduction

THE NEED TO IDENTIFY those responsible for the death of Jesus touches our humanity with as much cathartic, theological, and ideological force as the death of Jesus. Indeed, we often root our search for these guilty parties in our individual apologetic need; however, we must move beyond mere guilt-assignment for Jesus' physical death, because that death has moved past forensic understanding, as, after all, the body has long since vanished. From forensic matters, we must move into an assessment of what remains: the plethora of literary artifacts that pertain to guilt or cause.

The literary artifacts at our disposal are indeed vast. From recorded history and written traditions to social theories and other facets, there is virtually no shortage of material from which the researcher might draw. Through these documents we apprehend not only the cognitive environment of the New Testament, which formed the external environment in which Jesus lived, but also the way in which Jesus may have internally grasped his own identity.

From these literary artifacts about Jesus, scholars set forth a number of documents in which they sought to distill who the Jesus of history actually was. Often, these quests for the historical Jesus were driven by theological concerns and, as a result, became theological contributions themselves. This is true of many of these writings over the last two centuries. Certainly, the figure of Jesus is one of theology, rather than any historical fact—unless we are willing to alter our understanding of history. This is not to say Jesus was a myth or something other than a real person; but it is to say that what we have received of Jesus is theology more than it is history by our current understanding of those terms.

From this nexus of the quest of the historical Jesus, in addition to the literary artifacts described above, we have received a narrative about Jesus. Roland Barthes called this narrative, "international, transhistorical, transcultural: it is simply there, like life itself."[1] As Hayden White notes, the narrative is normally seen as only a *"form of discourse* which may or may not be used for the representation of historical events."[2] Because we have received not one but several narratives of the life of Jesus, including the final canonical chronicle, the person White determines as the "narrative historian" must learn to differentiate these narratives from one another, from the reception of the narrative, and, ultimately, from the author's initial narrative. They must uncover what happened before the events transposed to the medium.

If we are able to adequately take on the role of White's "narrative historians" and thereby accomplish this multilayer task of narrative differentiation, we will then be left not with just a historical person of Jesus sans theological interpretation, but what we hope is a more realistic person of Jesus: the Jesus of theology, drawn from the earliest possible theological narrative, from which the authors of canon in turn would have constructed their various narratives. Rather than denying the Gospel writers, and perhaps even Paul, the role of "historians," we should allow that they were simply translating their own "symbolic significances" into something of a theological stratagem.[3]

If we then concede the Gospel writers and even Paul wrote "histories," we may then allow each their own "emplotments," a literary device that encodes "the facts contained in the chronicle as components of specific kinds of plot structures."[4] Following this, we must then affirm each author—as a historian and theologian—built their own story on a previous narrative. Because of this, we may hear echoes of previous narratives and see cultural images reused (albeit with minor and unique changes) rather than a conclusive and original symbol. Yet, for all of this transforming of narratives,

---

1. Barthes, "Introduction," 79.

2. See White, "Question of Narrative," 1–33.

3. White writes: "Historical narratives . . . succeed in endowing sets of past events with meanings . . . the historian charges those events with the symbolic significance of a comprehensible plot structure" (White, *Tropics of Discourse*, 91–92).

4. White, "Historical Text as Literary Artifact," 223.

emplotment, and editorial work, one thing remains—virtually untouched at the center of the New Testament and early Christianity: Christ crucified.

The one generality most New Testament and Historical Jesus scholars can agree on without much nuance is the death of Jesus. Who he was, or thought he was; the facts surrounding, and significance of, the resurrection; and even the overall message, or messages, of his ministry have been and still are the topics of incessant debate, frequently resulting in as many conclusions as there are scholars. However, it is the death of Jesus that unites even the most diverse views of him. For example, Rudolf Bultmann argued for a historical account as the earliest report.[5] Helmut Koester believed, "there was certainly a written form of the Passion Narrative at an early date."[6] John Dominic Crossan, somewhat following Koester, went so far as to suggest the passion narrative was the original document from which the Gospels sprang.[7] Adela Yarbro and John J. Collins argue the death and subsequent resurrection formed the heart of the already existent argument that Jesus was in fact the long-promised Messiah. Ellen Bradshaw Aitken posited the death of Jesus constituted a central tenet of the Christian faith before Paul's ministry.[8] Centuries before these scholars, Justin Martyr called the cross the greatest symbol of the power of Christ.[9] Finally, the Apostle Paul considered his message one beginning with the cross upon which Jesus was executed (1 Cor 1:18). In summary of these many viewpoints, little doubt should remain that early Jesus followers treated the crucifixion of Jesus as the first and most important narrative of the faith. The death of Jesus generated not just what has become Christianity, but also the multifarious expressions and interpretations of those events. Indeed, all of these variegations drew inspiration from in the same emplotments.

---

5. Bultmann, *Synoptic Tradition*, 273, 275–79, 281. For more on this, see Aitken, *Jesus' Death*.

6. Koester, *Introduction*, 2:49, 163.

7. See Crossan, *Cross that Spoke*, 16–30. In this work, Crossan argues that a brief narrative of the crucifixion, lacking many of the elements found either in the canonical Gospels or the non-canonical *Gospel of Peter*, was all that the earliest Christians began with. Koester would respond to Crossan, arguing against a singular written source. See Koester, *Ancient Christian Gospels*, 216–30.

8. Collins and Collins, *King and Messiah*, 101–22.

9. Martyr, *1 Apology*, 55.

PROPOSAL

This study proposes to draw out a model not yet offered as completely as I believe it can be. I will attempt to present the death of Jesus not as one who was sacrificed unwillingly (passively, as if by others, namely God or the Romans, or alternately, the Jewish leaders); committed suicide in the modern sense as in time of mental distress; or suffered martyrdom; but rather as a premeditated *devotio*, albeit a *devotio* defined against the combined backdrop of Second Temple Judaism, Stoicism, and existing patterns of the Roman *devotio*. I will ask the readers to expand their understanding and reception of this model past what is sometimes and somewhat narrowly offered in recent scholarship, limited usually to an exchange made by Roman generals on behalf of their army. Rather, I will ask readers to expand their understanding—and hope to show why they are able to do so—of *devotio* to that of a death of a divine (see below) leader who does commit himself to death by his own free will in a contractual undertaking.

Defined simply, the *devotio* was a contractual self-sacrificing type of suicide. Those who commit the act *devote* themselves in death. Persons who executed the *devotio* did so neither for nor against a religious or political cause, but rather for a much deeper reason: to produce a significant change in the cosmic order that would result in an expected social peace. With respect to Jesus' death, each of the aforementioned views—sacrifice, suicide, and martyrdom—have been dealt with by scholars;[10] however, no such work yet exists explaining the death of Christ by the model set forth by Roman Stoics and initiated by Decius Mus, Cato the Younger, and the Emperor Otho among others—including Jews. Rather, such a view is often misunderstood as a "noble death."[11]

Further, I will propose death by *devotio* indicates not only a high Christological self- and communal viewpoint, but also, when paired with Judaism, it shows an elevated covenantal viewpoint. Indeed, had Jesus not thought of himself as God's son or the Davidic messiah, he would not

10. As will be discussed in later chapters, while their outcomes are the same, these three acts are different in intent. They cannot be confused.

11. For example, see Avemarie and Henten, *Martyrdom and Noble Death*; Droge and Tabor, *Noble Death*. I will cover the scholarship on "noble death" as a subset of self-sacrifice as viewed by both Romans and Jewish in subsequent chapters. Including Cato's suicide in this list is important as it is the one I will point to expand our current understanding of *devotio*. For others who list Cato as *devotio*, see Harrison, "Paul and the 'Social Relations.'" This topic will be explained further in chapter 4.

have completed the *devotio*, since only divine sonship and messianic self-identity can provide adequate motive for engaging in a *devotio* on behalf of the kingdom of God.

This is why we find this example used in Galatians. This type of self-sacrifice, which repeats itself throughout the New Testament, originates literarily with Galatians, a text that features this concept. Prolific, varied atonement models have led to a conflated maelstrom of hermeneutical confusion, and once the tempestuous sea of voices shouting various models is calmly silenced and the faithful reader is left alone to interpret the text, what will emerge—I believe—will be the earliest model for the atonement drawn from one of the earliest New Testament documents.

While the physical result—death—is the same in sacrifice, suicide, martyrdom, and *devotio*, the purpose and expected outcome are different. I will include *devotio* in the realm of suicide (self-inflicted death but not martyrdom).[12] Furthermore, I will only offer speculation as to the exact outcome of the calculus of life. Rational belief does not necessarily rest in provable facts and, as yet, we are unable to determine the precise consequence of either ending one's own life (suicide), or others ending one's life (sacrifice and martyrdom); therefore, I will speak only to what was said to have happened, or rather, the purpose of each change of reality as intended as believed by the individual who completed the act.

One will find a linguistic theme underpinning much of the New Testament, one which I maintain, is a latent deposition of the *devotio*. First of all, Paul used passive language in Romans 4:25 to describe Jesus as one who "delivered up for our sins" without strictly naming who or what led to this.[13] Likewise, in a statement clearly imitating Emperor Otho, Caiaphas hinted that the death of Jesus was a sacrifice (John 11:50) although Jesus earlier assured readers of the account that this sacrifice happened because he allowed and initiated it (John 10:18).

Further, we may read the startling example of Hebrews 10:19–20 which has long been recognized as connected, at least in verbiage, to the story of Decius Mus. Lucius Annaeus Florus wrote: "Who will wonder that

---

12. Jarvis Williams briefly examines *devotio* as a background to the Maccabean martyrdom, which is his proposed background to Paul's theology of atonement; however, while he can admit that the act has certain elements (expiation, appeasement, aversion of wrath, and a victim that is more than human) he passes over it as a similarity to martyrdom (Williams, *Maccabean Martyr Traditions*, 35–37, cf. 43).

13. For more on how this verse and how passive language plays a part in Paul's apologetic, see Linebaugh, *God, Grace, and Righteousness*; Dabourne, *Purpose and Cause*.

on this occasion the enemy yielded, when one of the consuls put his own son to death, though he had been victorious, because he had fought against his order (thus showing that to enforce obedience was more important than victory), while the other consul, as though acting upon a warning from heaven, with veiled head devoted himself to the infernal gods in front of the army, in order that, by hurling himself where the enemy's weapons were thickest, he might open up a new path to victory along the track of his own life-blood?"[14] This statement parallels the sacrifice found in the Hebrews passage, in that, just as Decius Mus sacrificed himself so that the Roman armies would have a literal way opened to victory against the Latin armies, so Christ's death and self-sacrifice in the midst of an otherwise hopeless situation opened up a spiritual way of victory against the hordes of hell, in order that believers might enter the presence of God. Even in light of these examples, in order to really begin the investigative work into the *devotio* as an early model, if not the progenitor of other models, we must turn to one of the earliest documented evidences of the death of Jesus: Paul's letter to the churches in Galatia.[15]

Concerning the dating of early Pauline correspondence, there is some dispute as to whether or not Paul wrote 1 Thessalonians before he composed Galatians. Both letters seem to have an early date. Ultimately, however, this discussion is irrelevant to our discussion for two reasons. First, Galatians was written to a regional group of churches while on the other hand 1 Thessalonians was written to a single church. Thus, Galatians exercised greater influence on a larger number of churches. Secondly, Galatians dealt with the foundation of the Pauline Gospel—Christ and him crucified—and with several topics directly related to the fruit of that foundation. 1 Thessalonians, by comparison, did not. Rather, with a much narrower scope, it exclusively dealt with a single issue not unrelated to the foundation of the Pauline Gospel—the return of Jesus. So, ultimately, even if the writing of 1 Thessalonians predates Galatians, Galatians was still the first of Paul's writings to work exclusively with the death of Christ on the cross, its meaning for those who follow him, and topics that naturally flowed out of that foundational topic. Because of this fortunate placement of Galatians

---

14. Florus, *Epitome*, 49. See also Attridge, *Hebrews*, 285n26; Dods, "Epistle to the Hebrews."

15. For the sake of brevity, I will follow Longenecker's date and audience measurements. See Longenecker, *Galatians*, lxx, lxxii–lxxxvii. He posits Galatians as earlier than 1 Thessalonians and written to communities in southern Galatia.

(as an early letter and as one speaking directly to the meaning of the death of Jesus), I will focus only on it for this work.

EARLY CHRISTIAN INTERPRETATION OF GALATIANS, APOSTOLIC FATHERS TO AUGUSTINE

While Galatians has become somewhat of a staple in theological interpretation since the Reformation, thanks in large part to Martin Luther's anchoring to it his challenge to Roman Catholic theology, its use in the early church was minimal when compared to Paul's other epistles. In this section, I will examine how patristic authors used and interpreted Galatians. I will limit the time period from the apostolic age to the time of Augustine, roughly four hundred years.[16] I will explore the patristic use of Galatians in three parts. In the first part, I will examine its usage by three apologists active from the end of the second until the beginning of the third century; while they did not leave us with commentaries on the whole epistle, their use of the epistle is important in understanding its place within the early Christian apologetic framework. Second, I will explore the commentaries of two late fourth-century theologians, Marius Victorinus and Augustine. Third, I will draw attention to the use, interpretation, and citation of Galatians 3:13 by a wide variety of Christian apologists and theologians. Given the use of this particular passage to the overall thesis of this current study, the exploration of how patristic sources read and used it, separate from the rest of Galatians, remains quite important.

Galatians as Theological Support

Irenaeus of Lyons (130–202) made slight use of Galatians to combat Marcion of Sinope, first in repealing the offensive dualism proposed by the church's first heretic, and second, as a subset of this first strategy, in building certain thematic doctrines (such as his Mariology) that showed the

---

16. For a discussion on Greek and Latin commentaries during this time, see Lightfoot, *Galatians*, 227–36. Lightfoot lists more than I will examine, but gives a good overview of the commentary's context. See also Souter, *Earliest Latin Commentaries*; Wiles, *Divine Apostle*; Turner, "Greek Patristic Commentaries," 484–532. For various citations of Galatians among early Christian writers, see Edwards, *Galatians, Ephesians, Philippians*. Two unpublished dissertations also help to highlight Galatians in the early church. See West Jr., "Ante-Nicene Exegesis;" Bechtel, "Exegesis of Galatians 2.14–21."

canon to contraindicate Marcion's teachings.[17] He was the first early writer to explicitly use portions of Galatians in his works, even though, as stated earlier, neither he nor other ante-Nicene writers provided commentary to the whole of the epistle. Using Galatians 4:4–5, Irenaeus built a significant bulwark against Marcion.[18] Also, he employed Galatians 1:1 to secure the validity of Church Tradition via apostolic succession.[19] This was similar to the argument Irenaeus employed when he used Paul's story in Galatians 2,[20] a story telling of a heterodoxy arising among the Apostles so that no one Apostle could treat themselves as sole arbiter of the Gospel's meaning. Along these same lines, Irenaeus utilized Paul's illustration of Abraham (Gal 3:5–6)[21] to state that the Christian faith was a direct continuation of Abraham's faith. In another place,[22] he used Galatians 1:15 to fight against the dualistic treatment of flesh and spirit, which treated spirit as the only godly and useful part of humanity, at the expense of treating the flesh as evil or worldly. Also, the writer used Galatians 5:19–21 to rail against his opponents.[23] Ultimately, however, Irenaeus did not attempt to use Galatians in any singular, systematic purpose. Rather, he used it in a proof-texting fashion, placing verses as they suited his purposes next to other sources in order to make the claim that the tradition of apostolic succession surpassed any new revelation, including Marcion's.

Like Irenaeus, Tertullian (160–220) did not provide a commentary, instead making use of Galatians in polemical discussions.[24] Unlike Irenaeus, however, Tertullian, utilized his knowledge of Latin rhetoric and oratory to more skillfully craft his polemic. Simultaneously, he afforded us the insight into a type of interpretation not yet covered in this study. Like Irenaeus, Tertullian heavily relied on Paul to combat Marcion's forced division between the God of Paul and the God of the Jews.[25] He accomplished

17. Irenaeus, *adv. Haer.* 5.21.1.

18. See Norris, "Irenaeus's Use of Paul" 79–98; Steenberg, "Role of Mary," 117–137, 119; Guthrie, "Irenaeus's Use of Galatians 4:4–5."

19. See Irenaeus, *adv. Haer.* 3.13.2.

20. Irenaeus, *adv. Haer.* 3.13.3.

21. Irenaeus, *adv Haer.* 4.21.1; 5.32.2.

22. Irenaeus, *adv. Haer.* 5.12.5; 15.3.

23. For one example, see Irenaeus, *adv. Haer.* 5.11.1.

24. For Paul in the second century, with a contribution focusing on Tertullian, see Bird and Dodson, *Paul and the Second Century.* For an anthology examining Tertullian's use of Paul, see Still and Wilhite, *Tertullian and Paul.*

25. It should come as no surprise that Galatians was Marcion's primary tool in

this first by showing that Paul was a Jew, and second, by showing that Paul was an Apostle, even if a lesser Apostle.[26]

The former of Paul's identities required the Roman lawyer use the Abrahamic imagery in Galatians 3:6–9 to show that the Christian message was a direct descendant to the faith of the Jewish patriarch.[27] Likewise, this allowed Tertullian to claim a singular cosmological reality for the Judeo-Christian tradition,[28] unlike Marcion's staged system.[29] Tertullian appeared to use *De praescriptione haereticorum* 33 as a sort of Pauline prophecy against the Eboinites while simultaneously maintaining, opposite Marcion and others, that Paul did have the full knowledge of the Gospel and nothing else was needed to enter into faith.[30] Finally, Tertullian was able to use Galatians as a way to introduce his hermeneutic framework. In *adv. Marc.* 3.5, he countered Marcion by using Paul's allegory of the two sons of Abraham (Gal 4:22–24), among other examples, to instruct others as to how to properly interpret Scripture.[31] Tertullian acceded to the heresiarch an almost correct view of Galatians. He allowed Marcion a great amount of interpretive room with Galatians. Indeed, Marcion, like Tertullian, viewed

---

attempting to wedge Paul away from the Apostles, and thus Jesus away from Judaism. See Tertullian, *adv. Marc.* 4.3.2–4; 5.2.1, for Tertullian's admission and reasoning as to why. See also Schmid, *Marcion und sein Apostolos*, 282–83, 294–96. Tertullian, like Marcion, was a supercessionist; however, unlike Marcion, Tertullian would see the continuity between Israel and the church.

26. For the former premise, see McGowan, "God in Christ," 5. For the latter, see Tertullian, *adv. Marc.* 1.20.2; *De praescr. haeret.* 23, as well as below. In *De praescr. haeret.* 23, Tertullian enforces the interpretation that Paul's rebuke of Peter was not a matter of doctrine, but one of how the doctrine should be carried out. Paul's reliance upon apostolic doctrine and his connection to the Apostles is maintained, even if Paul's status is muted somewhat.

27. This does not prevent Tertullian from acknowledging Marcion's claim regarding the anti-Judaism theme of Galatians (Tertullian, *adv. Marc.* 5.2.1). See Tertullian, *adv. Marc.* 5.3.2, one of Tertullian's longest continued use of Galatians, providing an interpretation for the *Sitz im Leben*, that of the Galatians returning, or turning to, the Law of Moses rather than the Gospel. Tertullian maintains that the Law was over, but it is over because the Creator sent Christ and in doing so, ended the law himself.

28. See Tertullian, *adv. Marc.* 5.2.7.

29. It is open to debate as to exactly what Marcion's cosmology was. See McGowan, "Marcion's Love of Creation," 295–311, for a balancing view of Marcion's cosmology as well as Lieu, *Marcion and the Making*.

30. See Scholer, "*Sed enim Marcion*," a paper delivered by the late Dr. Scholer at the Thirteenth International Conference on Patristic Studies in Oxford, August 16–21, 1999.

31. See Dunn, "Tertullian's Scriptural Exegesis," 141–55.

Galatians as polemical. Even with this allowance, however, Tertullian utilized his talents in logic and oratory in order to tightly define key terms and concepts of Galatians. He then furthered his argument by recasting several scenes in the epistle in order to produce an interpretation of Paul and his epistle that maintained a strong connection to the Jerusalem church, and thus to normative Christianity and Abraham, even while holding a supercessionist tension with Judaism.

Europe had Irenaeus and Northern Africa had Tertullian. Contemporary with these two men, yet dealing with different issues and living in a different region, Clement of Alexandria provided the land of Egypt with some excellent theological insights that incorporated Paul's epistle. For example, it is likely Clement used Galatians 3:23 as the impetus of his *Paedogogus*, as the first chapter of that work seems to indicate.[32] The theme of Galatians 3:23 also wove itself through *Stromata* 1.26, a segment in which the Alexandrian theologian, utilizing Galatians 3:19–23, built a case for seeing a connection between Abraham's faith and the Christian faith in the Law of Moses. In the words of Romans, another letter in which Paul makes connections between Abraham's faith and Christianity, this constituted a connection "from faith to faith."

Clement's usual employment of Galatians generally fell between two frameworks, with some exceptions. The first framework used Paul's statements on ethics as the basis for Clement's ethical exhortations. In this category, I would also include his views on sexual intercourse, which he considered ethical, especially in contrast to the writings of his detractor, Julius Casinos.[33] In *Strom.* 3.18, he used Galatians 2:19–20 not only to call for the faithful to engage ethical behavior but also to give the purpose for this ethical engagement.

For example, in *Strom.* 3.5, Clement explained, utilizing Galatians 5:13, that even though believers have been given the ultimate liberty by Christ, ethical living and a life in the context of self-control was the ideal use of the liberty that Christ has given us. The same applied to *Strom.* 4, in which Clement used Galatians 5:16–17 in much the same way as throughout chapter 5 to teach what the expected ethical behavior was, a quality he termed "manliness." Of course, ethical behavior, from his perspective was

32. See the note at *Paed.* 1.1 (Roberts et al., *Fathers of the Second Century*).

33. See Clement, *Strom.* 3.13, where Clement uses Gal 3:28. Clement's concern with validating the flesh against Marcion, Valentinus, and others appears in *Strom* 3.17, when he uses Galatians 3:3 to offer direct proof against Marcion that the dichotomy the gnostic had created was patently false.

connected to correct repentance, a critical quality that believers need to possess in order to avoid reaping what we have sown (e.g., the use of Gal 6:7 in *Quis. Div.* 4).

Clement's second framework used Paul's statements on the law both to connect Christianity to Abraham and Judaism, while showing (Greek) philosophy's "schoolmaster" role. Accordingly, law and philosophy will only bear fruit to the extent that they ground themselves in Christ.[34] In an exception that does not easily fit into either of the above two categories so easily, but remains germane, Clement did use Galatians 6:9–10 as self-justification for writing a number of other works and for validating the rightness of martyrdom.[35]

The First Commentaries on Galatians

While the early Church Fathers on one hand spent a considerable amount of time defending the Christian message from Gnostics through the use of fiery polemics and oratory, as seen above, the Apologists on the other hand demonstrated a preference for calm exposition of and expansion on the texts of Scripture to their audiences, which included gnostics and heretics. This method of handling the text led to the first commentaries on Scripture. Beginning with Pantaenus c. 180 in Alexandria, heterodox and gnostics both wrote commentaries to provide interpretations, usually against one another.[36] Clement, a student of Pantaenus, offered a brief exegesis of several passages in his *Hypotyposeis*, but this document has barely survived. While Tertullian's *adv. Marc.* 5.2–4 was often styled as a commentary of Galatians, it would not come close to Origen, the first notable

---

34. See Clement's use of Galatians 3:6–7 in Clement, *Paed* 1.11; *Strom.* 2.28, where he strives to show that law and faith are both united under the one God, because where as the law had led people to God, only faith (in Christ) can impart proper knowledge. He is resourceful in using Galatians 3:25 to support Galatians 3:12, 19 demonstrating that it is indeed the law, the very law despised by Marcion and other gnostics as well as the law cherished by the Jews, that leads to and ends in Christ. See Clement, *Paed* 1.6, 11; *Strom.* 1.26; 2.7–10. The apologist goes further, however, and places Greco-Roman philosophy on the same level of the Mosaic law, allowing that it acted for the Greeks the same way the law acted for the Jews. See his use of Galatians 4:1–3, 9 in Clement, *Strom.* 1.11; *Prot.* 5; 11.

35. For instance, see Clement, *Paed.* 3.12; *Misc.* 1.1

36. Before him, Papias was writing about the oral sayings of Jesus. See Eusebius, *Eccl. Hist.* 3.39, but Papias seems to refrain from reporting his own interpretation, saving the space for recording the sayings and who repeated them.

commentary writer.[37] Origen's work on Galatians, however, has been lost, albeit seemingly preserved, at least in passing, in Jerome's commentary (see below). Because space does not allow for it, and because some of the earlier commentaries have been lost, I will consider the first known and extant commentaries on Galatians: those authored by Marius Victorinus, Ambrosiaster, Jerome (who has preserved Origen's work), and Augustine.

Marius Victorinus (late fourth century), the first Latin commentator on Paul, was a Neoplatonist who converted to Christianity and subsequently carried his Neoplatonic philosophy into his interpretation of Scripture.[38] Only three of his commentaries on the Pauline corpus have been preserved: treatises on Galatians, Philippians, and Ephesians.[39] Except for Jerome, Victorinus's commentary on Galatians is the longest of this period. Alexander Souter speculated that this was partly due to the fact that Victorinus's commentary was the first in Latin, and one of his goals was to set this standard, a fact that remains true to present day.[40] Further, when compared to Ambrosiaster (who penned 36 Migne columns), and Pelagius (who wrote 19), Victorinus's 51 columns far surpassed the other two. The volume of columns demonstrates Victorinus's careful attention to detail.[41] In the absence of opposition, the commentator was able to delve into his interpretation of the letter's meaning. As one might expect, the former philosopher saw in

37. For this instance, I am defining commentary as a series of expositions of an entire canonical book. This should exclude Matthew and Luke or Tertullian's brief exegesis of the entire book of Galatians. Hypolytus of Rome is the first known author of a commentary, on the book of Daniel (written in Greek) while Victorinus of Poetovium's commentary on the Apocalypse is the first known commentary in Latin. See Cain and Lenski, *Power of Religion.*

38. For Victorinus as the first Latin commentator on Paul, see Mara, "Ricerche storico-esegetiche," 52. Giacomo Raspnati goes further, seeing Victorinus as the first Christian to explore a biblical text systematically. See Raspanti, *Mario Vittorino,* 81. For his Neoplatonic inheritance, see Clark, "Neoplatonism of Marius Victorinus"; Colish "Neoplatonic Tradition," 57–74; Haig, "Neoplatonism as a Framework," 125–45; Clark, "Neoplatonic Commentary"; "Psychology of Marius Victorinus," 149–66. See also Boin, *Coming Out Christian,* 113–20; Cooper, *Galatians,* 16–40.

39. See Copper, *Marius Victorinus,* 4; Souter, *Latin Commentaries,* 9–15.

40. Souter, *Latin Commentaries,* 21.

41. For comparison's sake, Jerome's commentary on Galatians is 130 columns. Unlike previous commentaries, Jerome may have tackled Galatians with such intensity (the sheer length of it, when compared to others of the time and even his own on other biblical books, shows the great importance Jerome placed on Galatians) that he may have helped validate the shift from the study of the Greek Old Testament to the Hebrew original. See Raspanti in Cain and Lössl, *Jerome of Stridon,* 163–71.

Paul a type of philosopher, and some passages of the commentary read as little more than philosophical soliloquies with a verse as prompt (for examples of this, see his comments on Gal 4:6; 5:19–6:2). However, there was a more pointed goal to Victorinus's writings: his exposition of the letter's theological underpinnings. In many sections, he highlighted this with the word *summa*. Like many modern commentators, the ancient scribe saw the letter's context for exactly as Paul seemed to say it, that the Galatians were slipping away from Paul's message back into a works-based Judaism.[42] His interpretation was solidly Nicene (cf. Gal 4:4), but overall, it did little more than paraphrase the Pauline primer.[43]

Ambrosiaster (writing c. 366–84) was an unknown author once thought to be Ambrose. However, since the late Middle Ages, he has come to be recognized as someone independent of the bishop of Milan. Indeed, the same author is now recognized to have given us three recensions of his commentary on the Pauline corpus.[44] While the identity of the author resides in the realm of rightful speculation, the context of the commentary does not.[45] A reading of the commentary reveals three things about the author: he is quite familiar with Jewish customs, aligned with Nicene orthodoxy, and lived in Rome.[46] Like Victorinus, Ambrosiaster would have recognized the traditional understanding of Galatians' context: a works-versus-grace rhetorical battle, with a "Judaizing force" on one side and Paul on the other.[47] Unlike Victorinus, there indeed appeared to be pointed

---

42. This is the *summa* of Galatians according to Victorinus as he writes in his prologue.

43. Raspanti, *Esegeta*, 98. See also Locher, "Formen der Textbehandlung," 137–43, with his allowance that commentator's paraphrase is a unique contribution, blending commentary and homily; Souter, *Latin Commentaries*, 22, who cares little for Victorinus; and Cooper who insists the commentator did concern himself with more technicalities such as grammar and textual issues (Cooper, *Marius Victorinus*, 100–1). Victorinus's work is important for numerous reasons, none of which seems to be what he actually said, but this seems to be goal. See his comments on Galatians 4:18 (Cooper, *Marius Victorinus*, 115).

44. Lunn-Rockliffe, *Ambrosiaster's Political Theology*, 11–32. See also Cooper and Hunter, "Ambrosiaster Redactor Sui," 69–91.

45. For a larger study on Ambrosiaster, see Souter, *Latin Commentaries*, 39–95. In this, he condenses and repeats much of his earlier study (Souter, *Study of Ambrosiaster*).

46. Bray, *Commentaries on Galatians*, xv–xvi.

47. Souter comments, "Probably no other commentator, Greek or Latin, realizes so clearly the attitude of the Jews to Paul and Paul to the Jews," (Souter, *Latin Commentaries*, 65). However, Ambrosiaster used Roman illustrations to sometimes make his point, following that of Tertullian, Clement of Alexandria, and Ambrose. This may help us below

opposition in Ambrosiaster's works, specifically against Photinus and the Manicheans (although he does mention more).[48] Further, in several passages, notably Galatians 3:19, Ambrosiaster pushed the interpretation to mean the following: that we have been liberated from the ceremonial law, that *sola fide* only refers to the baptism, and that *fides* will establish a *meritum*.[49] Ambrosiaster replaced allegorical interpretation with what arguably was a prototype of the historical method.[50] Accordingly, from his point of view, Christ was the liberator who rescued us from the failure to give reverence to God. Jesus did this by offering himself up (or surrendering) to the devil (Gal 1:4–5). To be sure, the ancient commentator did offer a different view on Galatians 4:24–26. Instead of making the chief dispute one between law and faith, he pitted Jews against Christians.[51] In doing so, Jesus not only saved his present followers but also descended to hell to recover those previously lost.

Eusebius Sofronius Hieronymus (347–420), or Jerome, continues as a person of interest, as he seemed to have preserved Origen's commentary on Galatians within his own, using it as a dialogue partner.[52] Thus, within Jerome's singular commentary, we have two—one commentary representing two authors, two languages, and two schools of thought.[53] Of special note is the following: Jerome took up Origen's previous use of Stoic definitions regarding ethical concepts.

For instance, Jerome drew his understanding of the ethics mentioned in Galatians 5:22–23 from Stoic thought, elsewhere seen as a method

---

in recognizing the allowance for such uses were made in the early church and often employed to explain Galatians. Or it may simply be a mode of speaking related to the new political realities of a Christian Rome.

48. Souter, *Latin Commentaries*, 64.

49. See his comments on 1 Cor 12:3; Rom 3:3, 20; 4; Gal 3:19. See Souter, *Latin Commentaries*, 79–81. Then see Ambrosiaster on Gal 3:27.

50. Souter, *Latin Commentaries*, 64–65.

51. For more on Ambrosiaster's familiarity with the Jews, see Speller, "Ambrosiaster and the Jews," 72.

52. According to Jerome in his letter to Paula (*Epistle 33*), Origen left fifteen books and seven homilies on Galatians—not to mention Origen's own *Stromata* that included a finely detailed examination of Galatians, clause by clause. Origen's *Stromateis* is mentioned several times by Jerome. See his introductions to book 1 and 2, Gal 1:11–12; 2:15; 5:13a, 19–21; 6:8.

53. Jerome was not the first, but near to the last, of the orthodox writers to make free and positive use of Origen. See Scheck, *St. Jerome's Commentaries*, 4–5.

Origen employed.[54] He also mentioned Cicero, who used Stoic thought in his writings on law and duty, several times, such as in Galatians 5:26.[55] This was not the last use of Stoic thought to find its way into Galatians via Jerome (and perhaps Origen) (cf. Gal 1:15–16a; 4:24). However, even though Jerome drew on Stoic reasoning for some of his commentary, in the second book of his commentary on Galatians he declared, somewhat hypocritically, that he did not want anyone but a Christian in "God's temple." This might beg the question, "why did he use them if he only wanted Christians in God's temple?" Perhaps Origen's sanitizing of the Stoics gave Jerome an incentive to utilize them, or perhaps Cicero's notion of a divine man escaped his scrutiny.[56]

Nevertheless, as with previous writers, Jerome situated Paul's epistle within the context of a conflict between grace and law, even if such themes were set within Jerome's context rather than Paul's.[57] In the introduction to Book 2, he even noted that the Galatians in his day still spoke the same language as the inhabitants of Trier, a city then inhabited by Celts, a point necessary to our overall discussion. In regards to particular themes, Jerome used Galatians to defend the freedom of the human will (Gal 5:8–12, 17)—themes defined more by Jerome than by Paul.[58]

Augustine (354–430), the well-known theologian and frequent compatriot of Jerome, wrote his systematic commentary on Galatians (c. 394) in a high, eloquent Latin. Quoting a small section of the text, he followed the quotation with his detailed view of the initial passage. What was unique about this particular volume of Augustine's literary legacy is the fact that Galatians was the only canonical book about which the Bishop of Hippo wrote any formal, systematic commentary. Also, he did not comment without interacting with other commentators. Pertaining to this interaction, he borrowed from Marius Victorinus on at least three occasions,[59] stood

---

54. Souter, *Latin Commentaries*, 121.

55. In this section, Jerome references Cicero's *Pro Archia Poeta* 11.26 and *Tusc Disp.* 1.15, 34.

56. Jerome's consternation about using non-Christian authors does not seem to matter after he utters the statement. See Souter, *Latin Commentaries*, 128–35.

57. See Jerome's commentary on Gal 1:3; 3:13–14; 6:2–5.

58. Several more recent scholars have labeled Jerome a "synergist." See Ferguson, *Pelagius*, 79–80.

59. See the two commentators at Gal 2:19; 3:1 as well as the use of the phrase "*spes salutis.*" See Plumer, *Augustine*, 28–33.

almost contra Jerome,[60] wavered between Hilary of Poitiers and Ambrose for moral authority and support, and highlighted Ambrosiaster positively.[61]

Certainly, as was the case with earlier-mentioned commentators, Augustine engaged with heretics by way of polemics. However, while the contentious nature of previous commentators was only passing and slight, Augustine's invective against opponents was overt and thematic. Conveniently, the text and context of Galatians lent themselves to Augustine's diatribe; he used the text and Paul's context as traditionally held to rally Christians against incoming heresies. Within the text of the commentary, Augustine neglected the exposition of background information, such as audience, historical purpose, and the Christological formula of Galatians 1:4, and instead moved directly towards using the text as a tool in his fight against heretics.

For example, he interpreted 2:9 against the usual (i.e., Jerome). Instead he saw this and other passages of the letter, such as 4:3, as prerequisites for Church unity. Further, he never wavered when he insisted that justifying faith was the same under both the Law and Grace. In insisting that we have been liberated from the Law, Augustine maintained that the Law, in light of our liberation from it, has only been interpreted wrongly but was not wrong of itself. This assertion of wrong interpretation accorded with Jesus' statement in Matthew 5:17, in which he claimed he came not to abolish the Law but to fulfill it, a principle he indeed fulfilled with his sacrifice. Indeed, Augustine's innovations were many, but the central discovery seemed to be united doctrine and ethics, themes which Paul covered extensively in the letter.[62]

Brief Analysis of Galatians 3:13 in Patristic Literature

Since Galatians 3:13 remains the focal passage of this work, and given the understanding that we will derive from it, it will be apt for us to examine this passage separately. For the most part, any brief analysis will demonstrate most patristic theologians who analyzed this text focused on what Christ became instead of the way in which he used what he became. Tertullian

---

60. This non-polemical discussion is centered on Gal 2:11–14. Plumer sees much of Augustine's commentary on this section of Galatians as a "negative reaction" to Jerome (Plumer, *Augustine*, 52–53).

61. See Mendoza, "Introduzione," 479–87.

62. Hays, "Christology and Ethics," 268–90.

used 3:13 several times in his defense against Marcion to show the connection between Jesus and the Hebrew deity, suggesting, for example, that Deuteronomy 21:13 was a prophecy about Jesus.[63] Using this fact, he attempted to trap Marcion logically by comparing his god against Tertullian's in applying the curse to Jesus.

Athanasius, writing in the middle of the fourth century, regularly used 3:13 as a defense of a high, non-Arian Christology. In one instance, Athanasius equated the curse of Galatians 3:13 with death[64] while in another, he likened the curse to flesh.[65] Gregory of Nazianzus suggested that Jesus only underwent an application of the curse,[66] which resembles the view John Chrysostom gave in his Homily on this verse. In it, he suggested Jesus took a curse so that he could then lift it. Ambrose would have agreed with Chrysostom.[67]

Of the first commentators, Victorinus is the only one who did not cover Galatians 3:13 other than in passing. He moved directly from 3:10 to 3:20, treating the "curse of the Law" in 3:13 as pertaining only to ceremonial rituals. However, at 2:20–21, Victorinus understood plainly that Jesus chose to hand himself over on our behalf and in doing so liberated us from the Law, which yielded a different life for the Christian. He saw the believer's obedience to Christ as the only right response due Christ; to do otherwise would be an ungrateful response "to the one who did so much for me, who for my sake would put himself in the line of fire in order to liberate me from my sins by taking their penalties upon himself."[68] Ambrosiaster went further by saying that the death of Jesus was a voluntary death, and in doing so became the curse needed to break the Law. He ended his commentary on that section by reemphasizing the role that the element of free will played in Christ's death, by giving it the purpose of placing Jesus on our side against the devil.

The words Jerome used in this Galatians 3:13 showed a great and faithful mind working to lay bare the authentic meaning of the Apostle—something he plainly found difficult given Paul's use of the LXX, a canonical

---

63. Tertullian, *adv. Marc.* 5.3.

64. Athanasius, *De inc.* 25.

65. Athanasius, *Contra Ar.* 2.47.

66. Gregory of Nazianzus, *Ep.* 101.61.

67. See *De fide* 5.14.178; *Ep.* 46.13; *Contra Aux* 25.

68. I have chosen to borrow Cooper's translation here given his use of the idiom. See Cooper, *Marius Victorinus*, 285.

interpretation almost forbidding the usual Christian interpretation, and the abhorrent suggestions established by Marcion. The amount of time and literary support he placed into this section causes the reader to consider how much Jerome struggled internally to determine the plain-sense reading of this single verse. Jerome split 3:13 into two sections, attaching the second clause to verse 14 in his examination. For 3:13a, he recognized Marcion's point but suggested Marcion held to this view precisely because he did not understand the original meaning of ἐξαγοράζω and thus only saw the vengeful demiurge, with the need to separate Jesus from this. Jerome went on to explain that the curse the Law brought on us was not God's doing, but was spoken of in a prophetic manner, that the curse was really a consequence of our reaping what we have sown (Gal 6:7). Jerome, somewhat following contemporary commentators, suggested Jesus became a curse (or a consequence) in order to alleviate the curse (or consequence) of not following the Law.[69]

While Jerome skillfully handled the first half of Galatians 3:13, it was in 3:13b–14 where Jerome struggled to make ends meet. He began by acknowledging the discrepancy between Galatians 3:13's use of Deuteronomy and the various Greek translations of Deuteronomy 21:22–23, namely the translation traditionally ascribed to the seventy, one to Aquila, another Symmachus, and other to Theodotion.[70] He examined the differences in translations, attempting to reconcile them to the original Hebrew. In one instance, Jerome quoted from a work no longer extant (*Debate of Jason and Papiscus*) in attempting to understand why Paul left off a phrase ("cursed *by God*") that appeared in many of the Greek translations, not to mention the Hebrew he knew so well as a Pharisee.[71] Jerome seemed to acknowledge that this phrase was original to Deuteronomy, but followed his Jewish instructor in understanding the phrase to mean the one hanged was to be

---

69. This understanding of curse as consequence fits into Jerome's total theology of heaven as reward. See O'Connell, *Eschatology of Saint Jerome*, 102–18.

70. Later in the section, Jerome derides Symmachus's translation, seeing in it a chance for Jews to slander Christians. Jerome is not content with this allusion in that particular translation of having blasphemy as the cause of the execution and goes far into proving, via canonical examples (often times creating logical pitfalls), that a mere hanging does not prove guilt.

71. This is one of the many times Jerome uses Origen as a source. See Harnack, *Der kirchengeschichtliche Ertrag*, 149. Given Jerome's use of Origen, often times without citation, the entire section could simply have as origin the Alexandrian teacher.

viewed as if it were God hanging on the pole.[72] In the end, he surmised only two possibilities, one that Paul wrote the sense of the words rather than the actual translation or that "by God" was added to the original by Jews intent on discrediting Christianity. In the eyes of those who would investigate Jerome while so far removed by the passage of time from the author, it would seem his struggle was never fully satisfied, for in the end he simply justified the absence of "by God" in Paul's quote by referring to the appearance of stupidity of the entire episode.

Augustine approached 3:13 plainly, seeing in this verse a suggestion Jesus did not uphold the law entirely, leading him to be the "curse." He wrote, "For this reason, while close to granting freedom to believers, the Lord Jesus Christ follow certain observances of the letter . . . and in doing so, incurred the hatred of worldly people and received the punishment for those who did not observe them so that he might set free all those who believe in himself." Augustine called this the *sacramentum est libertatis*, noting this verse was received differently among Jews, pagans, and heretics—and even among Christians. Only the spiritual could see it for what it was, as some Christians, he contended, believed this was referring to Judas. The bishop of Hippo then moved to read this verse through the lens of other Pauline passages (such as Rom 6:6; 8:3). Unlike Jerome, who wrestled with textual issues, Augustine has no time for such quibbles, and instead used his pastoral and theological expertise to prove Jesus was lifted up as the culmination of the events began by Moses in Numbers 21:9. For him, Jesus became a curse to end curses, death, and sin, "*Non igitur mirum, si de maledicto uicit maledictum, qui uicit de morte mortem et de peccato peccatum, de perpente serpentem. Maledicta autem mors, maledictum peccatum, maledictus serpens, et haec omnia in cruce triumphata sunt.*"

Summary

Early in the Christian apologetic tradition, Galatians existed only as a prooftext against Marcion who seemed to base his new vision of Christianity upon it. Because of this, early commentators used Galatians in a non-systematic function as a way to correct or rebut Marcion, rather than develop any actual theology from it. The first extant commentary of Paul's letter was by Marius Victorinus, who seemed to spur the commentary tradition in the West. Basing it upon non-Christian styles, the commentary developed

72. Scheck, *Jerome*, 139.

from the proof-texting of a previous generation to a formal apologetic of the intent of the book. It is quite possible that, without Marcion—who presented an arch-nemesis to Christianity even through Jerome's time—Galatians would have suffered severe neglect. As it was, precisely because of Marcion's heavy use—a misuse, orthodox critics would contend—we have serious thought and gravitas-laden writings devoted to Galatians, especially regarding the portions Marcion singled out as his defense against a Christian based on Judaism.

What we can gain from patristic commentators of any length is that Galatians 3:13 was a verse Marcion used to judge the Jewish deity, and to judge him rather harshly. We can also see how it became something of an embarrassment to Christianity exactly because of what it seemed to say—namely, that Jesus became sin, or a curse. No patristic commentator suggested Jesus was actually cursed. Augustine, however, came close to suggesting Jesus purposely committed sins, in order to extract the consequences, so that he could become the thing he was to destroy. All agreed the death was voluntary, that Jesus was *the* active actor rather than a passive one, with Victorinus and Ambrosiaster giving the heaviest weight to the fact that it had to be voluntary. What is apparent with the culmination of data presented is that Paul's words served to bolster Marcion but embarrass Christianity all the while giving theological strength to those who insisted Jesus' voluntary death ended the curse of the Law (however individual writers may have interpreted "curse").

PREVIOUS WORK ON AN IMAGE OF JESUS'S DEATH AS VOLUNTARY

There are several volumes examining the death of Christ from a standpoint of a Greco-Roman metaphor.[73] My focus, as stated above, is on a specific model that includes a particular theological viewpoint rather than metaphors.[74] *Devotio*, the model I will work with, is a religious act taking several

73. The three volumes I have in mind are Breytenbach, *Grace, Reconciliation, Concord*; Finlan, *Background and Contents*; Watt, *Salvation in the New Testament*. I would be remiss in not highlighting Hengel, *Atonement*, n6.

74. This is not precisely what is needed when examining a model, especially if the author states he is demonstrating the model before the audience. This is what Paul purports to do in his Epistle to the Galatians, to demonstrate the death of Jesus before their eyes. While he does use metaphors aplenty, I believe he is recalling a particular model, one perhaps even retained from even Jesus himself. As such, we must differentiate between

forms such as "self-sacrifice."[75] There are several types of this act, ranging from later Christian uses of piety to Cornelius Nepos's use in his *Alcibiades* when he writes, "*dissimulata nauseantis devotione.*"[76] I will limit my work here to three examples of modern authors speculating *devotio* may be at play in some parts of the New Testament.[77]

Royden Keith Yerkes, in connecting the votive, or freewill, offering to the *devotio*, found several instances of this in both the Jewish and Christian writings. He did so after laying a foundation from the Greek and Roman writings. He counted three specific instances of *devotio*—Jericho's destruction, the unnamed daughter of Jephthah, and Saul and Agag. He did this because he rightly saw that the death involved in each story was meant by the executioner to be received by the deity. Yerkes also believed *devotio*, if not for our English translations, could have been better seen in these stories. In the New Testament, *anathema* replaces *devotio*, hearkening back to a time in which the curse was used in a votive offering.[78]

Richard E. DeMaris challenged the image of sacrifice in the Gospel of Mark as applied to the death of Jesus, citing the contentious debate among scholars regarding the precise nature of a sacrifice. Dismissing the connection to the Passover and the cult of Israel, DeMaris favored the notion that images from Leviticus 16 may have filled Mark's mind. Consequently, this assertion requires us to view the death of Jesus as part of the "remedial or curative exit" rites existing at the time. DeMaris thus presented his audience with two rites that gave them and us new lenses for interpreting the death

---

metaphor and model.

75. H. S. Versnel has proposed two types: the *devotio hostium* and the *devotio ducis*. In the former, the victim was the enemy dedicated to the gods, while the latter the victim is the general. See Versnel, "Two Types of Roman *devotio*," 365–410. See also his article Versnel, "Making Sense of Jesus' Death," 213–94. In this latter essay, Versnel examines the death of Jesus, albeit from a rather wide angle instead of particular passages, via various definitions of "noble death" exhumed from pagan sources. He maintains his earlier stance on the *devotio*, limiting it to two, but does not connect the crucifixion to either Decius or Cato, mentioning these figures almost in passing.

76. Nepos, *Alc.* 6.5.

77. I am not the first to connect the *devotio* to the death of Jesus via the Roman models of Cato and Otho. Martin Hengel, in attempting to provide a Greco-Roman point of view to the crucifixion, does as well, albeit through a less defined *devotio* than I will present. As we will see, while atonement for sins or crimes were part of the motivation of the *devotio*, the act is more robust than Hengel summarized. See Hengel, *Atonement*, 23–24. His model, however, is still the traditional *consecration* involving *pharmakos*.

78. Yerkes, *Sacrifice*, 59–66. For his remarks on the erasing of *devotio* from our English translations, see Yerkes, *Sacrifice*, 66n31.

21

of Jesus: the *pharmakos* and the *devotio*. In turn, these interpretive lenses extended the reader's thinking towards considering Levitical purification rites.[79] These rites, as part of the Torah community's liturgy, were associated both with group crisis and the need to remove whatever evil was plaguing the community. DeMaris focused on the Gospel of Mark and suggested the Temple itself was the sacrifice.[80]

Basil S. Davis offered *Christ as Devotio, The Argument of Galatians 3:1–14*, which defined *devotio* as "a general term for the redeeming fine to be paid to the deity for the purpose of releasing the thief from the curse."[81] He argued that when Paul spoke of Christ "becoming a curse," he was picturing Jesus' as the penalty paid via *devotio*. For this aspect of "curse," Davis turned to the concept of *defixio*, or curse tablet. Christ's death paid a fine imposed by the curse that went into effect because humanity broke the Law of Moses. The Law itself was the curse, and this concept pointed Davis to the curse tablet. While his work was tied to this model, he admitted there was no example for a vicarious human sacrifice to fit his definition—no example of a *devotio* used to break a *defixio*—and turned to the military intention as exemplified by Decius Mus.[82] Davis did not examine the development of the *devotio* in Roman literature and thus did not offer parallels in contemporary Jewish works. Finally, he did not tackle the cosmological and anthropological properties of the *devotio*. Because of his flawed example, Davis overstated his case and thereby missed the Christological, anthropological, and cosmological aspects of the *devotio* and how this aids in interpreting Paul's message in Galatians.

If we allow *devotio* means in its simplest form, "a sacrificial and premeditated suicide,"[83] we can allow for an exploration of Christ's death as a

79. On the possibility of *pharmakos* as an image of Jesus's death in Mark, see Collins, "Finding Meaning," 175–96.

80. DeMaris, *Ritual World*, 95–110. He bases his example on John Kloppenborg's work, "*Evocatio Deorum*," 419–50.

81. Davis, *Christ as Devotio*, 166.

82. As one reviewer points out, Davis's example is "misleading" given the *devotio* was often used to place a curse and never to break one. See Scott, "Review of *Christ as Devotio*." See as well Mark Nanos's "Review of *Christ as Devotio*," 335–37. This is not the limit of Davis's issues. He misreads the military *devotio* to mean it is removes a curse upon an army, a view any classicist would disparage. He ignores Deuteronomic theology (Deut 27:26; cf. Gal 3:10) so that Paul is more of a Roman than a Jew in view of curses.

83. The term "suicide" is a relatively new concept; the idea of a taking one's life for issues not related to honor, or any of the other ancient reasons, is even newer. However, I believe the anachronistic term is best and will be used periodically given its emotional

form of *devotio* even if the proper term is not used. With this in mind, we turn to two authors, one making use of the other. Jack Miles, in his seminal work, *Christ: A Crisis in the Life of God*, posited the death of Jesus as a suicide.[84] It is the account of God who had abandoned Israel but returned to keep his promise as it was his character to do so. To do so, God became human in the person of Christ.[85] Miles used Pierre-Emmanuel Dauzat's work, "*Le suicide du Christ: Une theologie*," to buffer his work. In this work, Dauzet called attention to Christian scripture, emphasizing the Gospel of John, to show that treating the death of Jesus as a suicide was a viable interpretation. However, going further, Dauzet states, "*L'idée du suicide du Christ aura été avant toutes choses une idée de chrétiens, sinon une hypothèse christologique*."[86] While Dauzet's work focuses primarily on the Gospel of John, he does include a brief excursus into Paul's work. He noted the grand paradox in Paul's writings: that we are to not only imitate Jesus completely by dying, but also by living. For the paradox, he offered Philippians 2:7 and Galatians 2:20 as part of his resolution. He writes,

> Si l'apôtre Paul a raison et que le vrai sacrifice est bien de rester vivant, la théologie sacrificielle c'est trompée d'objet: le sacrifice du Christ, c'est se vie. Son don, c'est sa mort, à commencer par la mort qu'il se donne. A cet égard, le repprochement avec Antigon est necessaire, car les évangélistes ont créé un Jésus mort de son plein gré, de son propre chef, sinon de sa propre main. Et ce geste est necéssairement positif.[87]

If we understand that Paul's imitation paradox was resolved if we see that the imitation requires us now to live exactly because the death of Jesus was voluntary, we reach a simple conclusion. We carry in ourselves the life

---

charge and his direct connotation of free will.

84. The possibility of seeing Jesus's death as a suicide has been raised, in fear, by Catholic theologians, such as Robert L. Barry who insists that only a wide definition of suicide would allow for that as the case. See Barry, *Breaking the Thread of Life*, 1.

85. Miles, *Christ*.

86. "The idea of the suicide of Christ will have been before all things an idea of Christians, if not a Christological hypothesis (Author's translation)" (Miles, *Christ*, 164–67). See Dauzet, *Le suicide du Christ*, 1.

87. "If the Apostle Paul is right and the true sacrifice is to remain alive, sacrificial theology is deceived: the sacrifice of Christ is life. His gift is his death, starting with the death he gives himself. In this respect, the return with Antigon is necessary, because the evangelists created a Jesus dead of his own free will, on his own, if not his own hand. And this gesture is necessarily positive" (Dauzet, *Le suicide du Christ*, 62. Author's translation). For a full discussion, see Dauzet, *Le suicide du Christ*, 59–64, 69.

of Jesus only if we fully imitate him. Just as Jesus chose death and received life as a result, now the Christian must choose life, which comes likewise through death to self. Through Dauzet's writings, his audience saw Paul as the first expositor of Jesus's forceful voluntary death.

While the death of Jesus has been explored somewhat as a *devotio*, that is, as a self-sacrifice via suicide, it has yet to be explored via the lens of a refracted model as offered by Cato the Younger and the Emperor Otho.[88] Both of these men committed the *devotio*, not to some lower deities as Decius Mus was said to have done, but to provide for an end to the disorder brought about by a civil war. With *devotio* as offered by Cato and Otho, anthropological characteristic emerges—namely, the free will of the victim to choose death—and mixes with the Christological aspects, in order to show an early and high view of the divinity of Jesus. What the reader missed from previous research was the logical end to a self-inflicted death of Jesus. The suicide of Jesus could only happen because of free will, worked only because of whom he thought himself to be, and served a higher purpose than that usually afforded to other victims of self-inflicted death.[89] Finally, it was premeditated, with the hallmarks of a planned suicide.

PROPOSAL SUMMARY

How should we best understand the death of Jesus as presented in Galatians? If we can identify the proper model, it can provide us not only with an apposite mechanism to understand how the covenant is renewed for Israel and how salvation is enacted for the Gentiles, but also how to read the rest of the letter. The proper image of the death of Jesus then becomes the interpretative key for the letter if not early Christology.

---

88. I am not the first to connect the display of Cato's death in Lucan's *Pharsalia* to the review of the Cross. Martin Hengel, in attempting to provide a Greco-Roman point of view to the crucifixion does as well, albeit through a less defined *devotio* than I will present, does so but only through the mirror of a vicarious sacrifice As we will see, while atonement for sins or crimes were part of the motivation of the *devotio*, the act is more robust than Hengel summarized. See Hengel, *Atonement*, 23–24. His model, however, is still the tradition *consecratio*.

89. The death of Jesus, rather than existing in a cosmological reality (such as whether or not a victim achieves a reward in the after life), is cosmological in goal, or, rather, the death of Jesus is meant to effect cosmological change. By "worked" I mean Paul's understanding as well as the early Church. This is not a scholarly assumption of the mechanism.

My thesis will suggest a particular model of *devotio*, one focused on dying to achieve peace through the end of a conflict rather than a sacrifice aimed at achieving victory, is the model used not only in the epistle, but so too in the New Testament.[90] I will show Galatians easily associates with this model, dependent heavily upon 3:10–14; however, my reading is not limited only to this passage in Galatians but is drawn from the rest of the book as well. Likewise, because this type of *devotio* is performed, this will help to explain Paul's terminology of ἐλευθερία and his view of the free will of Christ in self-sacrifice as well as the "new creation" (6:15). Finally, I will demonstrate that the earliest Christology is a high Christology, with the *apotheosis* preceding the sacrifice. I believe this is the original narrative of the death of Christ, of self-sacrifice of the divine meant to renew the covenant while bringing an end to the eschatological crisis.

RESEARCH QUESTIONS

The death of Jesus continues to raise questions, and all the more so when one suggests it may likely have been a premeditated one, by his own hand. Historical Jesus research has focused on the apologetics needed to present a crucified bandit as messiah, especially in light of a successful Roman campaign and subsequent destruction of the Temple. Yet, Paul wrote before that portion of history but successfully aided later apologists, such as the Evangelists, to continue skillfully crafting the story of Jesus for later crucial events. How did Paul present the death of Jesus as a self-sacrifice? Further, if he did so in a region known for human sacrifice, how did he separate the death of Jesus from the pagan contributions? Simply, Paul had to work to answer the Jewish and Roman reactions to self-inflicted morality. Further, Paul had to make sure of certain known emplotments, models of *devotio*, to tell his story. In doing so, he could not stray too far from previous models nor from what he understood to be the truth of the death of Jesus. All of these entanglements call us to consider, how is the Jesus's death portrayed in Galatians 3:1–14, specifically 3:13? Does a well-defined model of *devotio*

90. While peace may result from a military victory, and thus this argument looks merely like a word play or a battle of semantics, it is not. Rather, the peace achieved via my model of *devotio* is not one concerned with a momentary battle, but one whereby the victim seeks to, through his own death, achieve an equal peace in the face of a defeat that has already taken place. For example, the Emperor Otho, who once learning of the defeat of his forces by Vitellius, committed the *devotio*. This was certainly not about achieving victory but about achieving peace and bringing an end to cosmological crisis.

help us to read the death of Jesus and the entirety of the Epistle to the Galatians?

CHAPTER OUTLINE

To answer these questions, I will divide this work into two parts. In the first part, I will examine the social contexts of Paul's letter to the Galatians (chapter 2) and Jewish views of a death by choice (chapter 3). Chapter 4 will examine the *devotio*; chapter 5 is a brief introduction to the modification of Christian views of self-death during the same time period as explored above; chapter 6 will intend to bring the information together.

While I briefly discussed Jewish and Roman views of human sacrifice in this introduction by way of introducing the purpose of this study, I will explore each of these viewpoints in a subsequent chapter in larger detail. It is clear Paul and the authors of the canonical New Testament saw themselves as fulfilling the literary tradition of the Jewish books. Therefore, I will seek to establish views of human sacrifice in the Jewish canon as Paul's primary model, but leave space for Paul to have used, to aid his readers, a Roman model. These chapters will also include a deeper examination of Jewish and Roman views of self-sacrifice to reveal whether or not the intention of the victim was considered in judging the sacrifice as these viewpoints factor into the interpretation of Jesus becoming a curse.

The goal of these studies will be to establish the *devotio* as a model of self-sacrifice recognizable by both Jews and Romans, a model including specific expectations not only of outcome but also of the victim itself. These, along with the Christian view, will serve as my *ratio decidendi*. It is not that later Christians worked to cover-up the death of Jesus as one made by his own choice, but that it slowly became muted as Christian Tradition reacted against the *schismata*. It simply became less acceptable to see the voluntary death of Jesus as a self-death, especially when the cult of martyrdom turned into suicide pacts, and it became more acceptable, more preferable, to first blame the Romans and then the Jews.

In the second part, I will begin by exploring the many uses of *devotio* in Roman literature. As Davis and DeMaris have shown, *devotio* as self-sacrifice was known during the time of Jesus; however, as I have stated, previous scholars did not fully explore the range of *devotio* types. They either gloss over the range of types or assign it to a known category, such as martyrdom.[91] I will provide examples relevant to the time period to offer a particular type of *devotio*, establishing context and purpose of the act—while separating it from current views that it is simply another form of martyrdom. In chapter 2, I will explore the social science context of the audience, including the role arena and sacrifice may play in Galatians, along with the role Stoicism played in the formation of the theology of the New Testament writers. This will help us in reading the Christological and cosmological attributes in Galatians along with setting them in their proper context.

In chapter 6, using the definition of *devotio* established in chapter 4, I will present a reading of the Epistle to the Galatians. This chapter, the crux of the work, is divided into two parts. The first part will establish 3:1–14 as the mechanism of the salvific event. Since the death of Christ is pictured here as a *devotio*, we understand Paul held a high Christology and a cosmology based on πίστις Χριστοῦ. The model does not merely function as a "how-to guide," but the actual mechanism used to honor the covenant and to secure the salvation of the Gentiles. The examination of these traits throughout the whole of Paul's epistle is contained within the second part of this final chapter.

VALUE OF THIS WORK

The value of this research is first to better define *devotio* to include *apotheosis* and thus point to an early Christology higher than what many modern critical scholars have allowed. Second, this model helps to explain the early success among Gentiles. I believe that if this model were the one used by Paul not only in a public demonstration but also in his earliest preaching, it could have possibly come from Jesus himself. While this seems an august statement, if the *devotio* was in view then the model requires certain elements I believe have been missing from various debates about the atonement and the historical Jesus—namely, Jesus' would-be intentional self-harm. Third, such a model—a model that includes historical examples and a social-scientific background—will make better sense of the entirety of Galatians, establish a theological trajectory for the early Church, and

---

91. Di Berardino is correct. "It was not always easy to distinguish clearly between martyrdom and suicide. Jesus taught that the giving of one's life for one's friends was the greatest sign of love (John 15:13); the gospel of John insisted on affirming that Christ's death was voluntary" (Di Berardino, "Suicide," 650).

integrate various aspects of Galatians often examined independently of the death of Jesus as portrayed in 3:13.

I intend to show certain basic assumptions in Paul's theology—especially Christology—are not his creation, but one consistent with Roman and Jewish models and expected with the figure of Jesus' death I believe enshrined in the Pauline image of the Cross promoted in Galatians and one found in the early Church. Paul did not create a high Christology, nor an individual's death providing for an atonement of sins. Perhaps Paul captured this idea from his social context. Rather, I believe the social context cemented the Pre-Pauline language, deriving if not from Jesus, than from those who witnessed the death of Jesus—from those who had walked with Jesus.

Chapter 2

The Social Science Contexts

INTRODUCTION

IN THIS CHAPTER, I will examine the cognitive milieu of Paul's letter to the community in Galatia. We have to remember Paul is a transporter of the early Jesus tradition while understanding himself to be the apostle to the Gentiles, a mission and position equal to that of Peter (Gal 2:8). Because of this, the background for the letter must include several components. First, the religious syncretism of the Jew and the various versions of the Gentile cult must be assessed. This requires us to examine the syncretism of the Roman cult with the native Galatian cult. Since the area of Galatia has a long history within the Roman Empire, this too must factor in. Paul is not merely writing to an unambiguous group of Gentiles, but to a specific ethnic group who share many similar experiences to that of the Jews. He was also writing as a Jew with a particular Greco-Roman background and as he demonstrated in other letters, a particularly educated background.

While there are many avenues to explore the social-scientific background of Paul, the people of Galatia, and the letter he wrote, I will limit it to specific areas that concern *devotio* and how it transforms Paul's thought. After reviewing the cultural context of the Galatian Gentiles, I examine whether or not it is allowable to have a Jew writing to Gaulish Gentiles while formulating some sort of Judeo-Roman syncretism. After all, the *devotio* is a specific Roman method of suicide but Paul is using it to justify the death of the Jewish messiah.

Second, I will examine the possibility of an influential imperial cult and civic ritual in the province of Galatia. Following this, I will examine the role human sacrifice, an explicit civic ritual, was allowed in this *koinon*. Because the model of the *devotio* I will propose is based on Cato the Younger and the Stoics, I will then explore Stoicism as it relates to the New Testament and Paul specifically as well as the epistemological role testimony (Gal 1:20; 4:15; 5:3). All of this is done to show that the cultural milieu allows for a rich expression and turning emplotments, such as the one I will propose.

THE PEOPLE(S) OF GALATIA

The people of Galatia were hardly homogenous, a fact that matches the scholarship debate regarding the cultural grouping of the audience of Paul's letter. David Rankin, a scholar of the Celtic peoples, writes, "there is nothing identifiably Celtic" in many of Paul's admonitions. Further, he sees no "overtone of racial prejudice" in the vaunted phrase of Galatians 3:1.[1] Graydon Synder, on the other hand, disagrees and sees nothing of an exilic reception by the Irish diaspora for the letter.[2] Due to Galatians 3:1 and the lack of Jews in Paul's congregations, Martyn argues that the peoples to whom Paul is writing were heavily Celtic.[3] However, as Rankin has shown, far from the mental image "Celt" brings to mind, the inhabitants of Galatia were heavily Romanized, some tendencies to find affinity with the Stoics.[4] This Romanization may be attributed to the use of a first-century BCE Celtic chieftain's alliance with Rome to unite the various tribes under him.[5] By the time of Paul's letter, while Celtic influences would have remained and been known—especially by the ruling elite—the peoples of Galatia were Roman, and as evidenced by the Roman geographers and historiographers of the time, still gave the Empire something to fear.[6]

---

1. Rankin, *Celts and the Classical World*, 205.

2. Synder, *Irish Jesus, Roman Jesus*.

3. Martyn, *Galatians*, 16. This view is supported by others as well. See also de Boer, *Galatians*, 4.

4. Rankin, *Celts*, 79–81.

5. Asano, *Community-Identity*, 22.

6. "(Galatians) is a term soaked with memories, fears, and aggression that are completely absent from our New Testament dictionaries. Firmly established on the ideological map of the Roman Empire as barbarian territory par excellence, it is a worldwide topos that inscribes the history of a dramatic and paradigmatic encounter between Rome and its enemies, the history of the conquest of lawlessness by law" (Kahl, *Galatians*, 51).

For the purpose of this reading of Galatians, it is not necessary to distinguish completely the tribe of origin for Paul's audience. Rather, I will follow Martyn, et.al, in reading the people as primarily Celtic in distant-origin, but note that due to the generations spent under Roman occupation, along with forced political mergers with other tribes, and the natural syncretism developing during such a time, that the people retained Celtic emplotments aided and understood by Roman realities.

Judeo-Roman Syncretism

It has become increasingly fashionable to consider the Greek influences upon the New Testament, which is a natural occurrence given the original language of the corpus. We cannot afford to limit the creation of the New Testament, nor the genesis of the viewpoints espoused in the New Testament to the mythical world of a purely Jewish tradition; however, if we ignore the direct weight of the Jewish literary and theological tradition it will lead us into a debt of disconnect in which we have a purely Greek, or Roman, Jesus sans Moses, Elijah, or any of the prophets. Rather, we must take the early attendants to the story of Jesus as a confluence of Jewish and Roman influences, even if—and especially if—they relied heavily on their Hebraic ancestry. As such, in examining various atonement models, among other theological precepts found in the New Testament, it has become helpful to consider other options in the formation of the intellectual structure of the worldview of the author. With this, we must allow that other legends and myths of the Roman world surrounding even Hellenistic Jews served, if nothing else, to influence the language used in the earliest Christian apologetic.[7]

Such a confluence may more easily, and with a solid methodology, explain the acceptance of the crucified Jewish messiah among the Gentile populations. As Martin Hengel explains, "The Gentile who heard the gospel was quite familiar in his own way not only with the hero's self-chosen death as a way to apotheosis *per aspera ad astra* and the theme of vicarious

While not siding with a solely Celtic-reception, Witherington does provide us with a middle ground. See his discussion on the recipients in Witherington, *Grace in Galatia*, 2–4.

7. For those who have made the argument to explore New Testament theology within the realm of this middle ground of Jewish and Greek sources, see Wengst, *Christologische Formeln und Lieder*; Hengel, *Atonement*; Seeley, *Noble Death*; Williams, *Jesus' Death as Saving Event*.

dying for others out of love, but also with the notion of a voluntary death as an atoning sacrifice, and he could have also understand it in his own way."[8] If this is the case, and I believe it is, then we would do well to continue to explore the full realm of the images of an atoning sacrifice as we seek to explain the reception of the death of Jesus in both the Jewish and the Greco-Roman worlds.[9]

Recent Scholarship on the Imperial Cult and Galatians

With the act of the *devotio* seemingly drawn from Roman sources, it behooves me to mention the current state of scholarship around the imperial cult and the Epistle to the Galatians. While I will not pass judgment on the rise and use of empire as a lens in reading the New Testament, mainly in American scholarship, one must remember the use of an image found in other cults does not mean Paul is using it to counter or otherwise overtake the previous cult.[10] While *devotio* as an image is one primarily associated with Roman imperial ideology, I maintain this does not mean Paul used it as an argument against Rome. However, it is necessary to examine recent scholarship, if for nothing else but to show Paul's audience would have at least known the religious and political implications of the image.

In recent decades, there have been two major works examining the connection of the imperial cult to the epistle. The first is *Galatians Re-Imagined* by Brigitte Kahl, a work removing the Judaism of Paul's opponents, replacing it with a juxtapose against Roman views of law and order.[11] The second work, *Galatians and the Imperial Cult*, sees the argument of Galatians something akin to a civic camouflage.[12] Rather than delve into the merits and conclusions of their argument, I will examine their evidences of

8. Hengel, *Atonement*, 28.

9. For examination of Paul as a Jewish-Greek interpreter in a Greco-Roman world, see Hengel and Deines, *Pre-Christian Paul*.

10. For two competing theories on a New Testament imperial agenda see Horsley, *In the Shadow of Empire*; McKnight and Modica, *Jesus Is Lord, Caesar Is Not*. Both works mention Galatians, but only in passing or as part of a larger topic on Paul's imperial lens.

11. Kahl, *Galatians Re-Imagined*.

12. Hardin, *Galatians and the Imperial Cult*. See Elliott, "Apostle Paul and Empire," 106. Elliot spends little time on Galatians, but in one paragraph tries to position the lineage of Abraham against that of Augustus (much as Kahl does in her work). His position is that the new converts in Galatia were attempting to use Judaism as a cover to avoid participating in imperial cult.

the imperial cult with the corollary that context does not mean argument, rather only serves as an allowance for the use of known images.

Kahl avoids the distinction between North and South as the province of the letter, going much further and connecting it to the whole of the Gaul-Galatia bloodline. She bases this on history as well as the linguistic plight in not separating the Gauls inhabiting the area now known as France and the descendants of the Celtic diaspora occupying an area in Asia Minor as well as a post-Constantine interpretative strategy she abhors. After promoting her view by using binaries and other linguistic turns, Kahl finally delves into re-imagining Galatians. She removes the Jewish ethnocentrism that is the usual exegetical framework only to replace it with the visual images of the Great Altar of Pergamon.[13] Because of this, she is able to then compare each statement by Paul against Roman images of somewhat equal standing. For instance, God is juxtaposed against the Emperor while the freedom promised by the Gospel is contrasted with Roman (and not Jewish) law. Of course, as usual with Empire critics, "gospel" becomes solely the answer to the Emperor's news of victory. Kahl adds to the discussion of the possible imperial cult in Galatians only what we already know: that as a Roman province, it was prevalent. However, she does add the ability to see cultic images in Galatians, even if the *caol áit* are too thin.

One particular image is the use of gladiatorial games as a form of human sacrifice. As often is the case, Kahl begins with the Great Altar where the images of human sacrifice are explicit and then moves to Galatians. She notes the arena is bereft of the usual connotations of ritual sacrifice such as the absence of priests and the need for the community to be reconciled with the deities. However, what are present are segregated spaces, a well-regulated public stage, mythological overtones of blood, and the act of a sacrifice meant to bind the community together. She notes, "the games can be seen to have a cathartic effect by vicariously eliminating violence and evil dwelling not only outside but also inside the social body, for example, in terms of slave or gladiatorial rebellions, treachery, and *civil wars* (emphasis mine)."[14] The battle becomes a sacrifice to purify the community of violence, reuniting the community after a struggle. That the Galatians

---

13. For instance, Kahl attempts to compare Paul's prologue (Gal 1:1–9) with the physical image of the Great Altar (Kahl, *Re-imagining Galatians*, 246–47). It is based on the imagery of war and wrestling.

14. Kahl, *Re-imagining Galatians*, 163.

were not foreign to human sacrifice is forever recorded by Diodorus.[15] The act of human sacrifice had become abhorrent to the Romans, but was still welcomed and proclaimed among the Galatians.[16]

Justin K. Hardin's work fleshes out the imperial cult, adding another dimension. Hardin writes, "It is clear that often the public worship of the emperor, rather than supplanting the local pagan religions in the Greek East, was simply amalgamated with it."[17] Galatia was a unique province within the Roman Empire. Augustus colonized both north and south, although the southern portion of the province required quelling (c. 5 BCE).[18] Because of this, unlike other Greek ruling cults brought in with various new rulers, the Roman imperial cult began by Augustus, moved into all realms of the public and private life exactly because it was designed to.[19] It "superseded traditional religious worship with a uniform system of religious devotion" binding the colonized lands with the Emperor, rather than other forms of Roman religion. While the people inhabiting the province of Galatia had long roots back to Gaul, with those roots transporting and preserving their native religion, their indigenous deities and temples were replaced (at least in importance) with the Roman ritualistic caste. For instance, Pessinus, while often thought to be the temple of Cybele (who will factor into our discussion later) is devoted instead to the Roman cult.[20] While this substitution took place, the people of the province were able

15. Kahl connects the human sacrifices of the Gauls/Galatians to the sacrificial act of sacking Rome as well as the sanctuary of Apollo at Delphi (Kahl, *Re-imagining Galatians*, 42–43). Of a particular note is the sacrifice of a Galatian man and woman (as well as Greek pairing) twice in Rome during the Second Punic War in a *devotio* meant to save the city from devastation. Hannibal, the threat to Rome, never managed to sack Rome, but would soon find Carthage itself sacrificed to the gods in the place of Rome. See Reid, "Human Sacrifices at Rome," 34–52; Várhelyi, "Specters of Roman Imperialism," 277–304.

16. Kahl suggests Nero reenacted the return to human sacrifice on behalf of easing social tension and creating a new social order (or city, in this case) when he charged the Christians with setting Rome on fire (Kahl, *Re-imagining Galatians*, 296).

17. Hardin, *Galatians and the Imperial Cult*, 40. Unlike either the Roman imperial cult or the indigenous Celtic cults, Judaism was not local, but rather focused back to Jerusalem.

18. Hardin, *Galatians and the Imperial Cult*, 49, 56.

19. Hardin, *Galatians and the Imperial Cult*, 47.

20. Hardin, *Galatians and the Imperial Cult*, 41. See also Waelkens, "Imperial Sanctuary at Pessinus," 37–72; Devreker et al., "Imperial Sanctuary at Pessinus," 125–44.

to avoid assimilation. Even at the Pessinus temple, Celtic priests still performed rituals making use of both Rome *and* indigenous cultic aspects.[21]

While both Kahl and Hardin go on to reinterpret Galatians in light of the surrounding provincial imperial cult they see, they both fail to make use of the non-assimilationist stance held by the non-Jewish population of Galatia. If the native religion could prevent assimilation, then it is more than likely the Jews (with their imperial protection) would not feel the overall pressure as both Kahl and Hardin suggest they do, even a new sect within Judaism.[22] However, what both show is that the imperial cultic images were prevalent in Galatia while not acting as a major threat and at times were themselves transformed to aid the local religion. This allowed other images to be used in dialogic currency. Further, while Hardin does not focus on it, Kahl does mention the very visual presence of human sacrifice in the public arena, and it is a sacrifice used for both civic and cultic binding. Finally, neither sees the death of Christ as any particular theological or ideological turn in Paul's letter; it is simply there.

PAUL'S USE OF SPECTACLE AND SPORTS METAPHORS

Given that this present study is largely dependent upon Paul's ability to use emplotments relevant to his audience, and thus an acceptable and provable transference of semiotic cues, we must first determine if Paul (and his spectators) used metaphors related to the spectacle. It is my assertion he did and as such, I will briefly examine such symbols in the Pauline corpus, first to identify Paul's use as well as an expectation that his audience (as well as the general Pauline corpus audience) would have understood them, given the frequency of use. While I do not consider the Pastorals or Ephesians and Colossians as authentic to Paul as a necessary point to argue given their authors expected to appeal not only to the authority of Paul, but so to the audience of Paul's authority, I will assess their uses of spectacle and sports metaphors as secondary support to the overall hypothesis that Paul

---

21. Hardin, *Galatians and the Imperial Cult*, 69. Hardin mentions the use of sacrifices performed by the priests, much as Kahl above. While not as clear as Kahl, Hardin notes that the Temple had as part of its complex a Roman-style arena. These priests would provide gladiatorial games and other hecatombs during their tenure, allowing the priest to offer sacrifices that combined civic and cultic intents. See Mitchell, "Galatia under Tiberius," 17–33. See also Stephen Mitchell's work showcasing the syncretism between Rome and Gaul in Galatia (Mitchell, *Celts in Anatolia*).

22. Hardin, *Galatians and the Imperial Cult*, 102–10.

not only used the images, but the understanding of what the phrases meant was accessible to a wide audience.

The verb τρέχω is a favorite image in the Pauline corpus. Rather than the nominal meaning of a swift walk, it has connotations of the stadium where prizes were awarded for an athletic feat of endurance. In Philippians 2:16, it is directly connected to the sacrifice (σπένδω) Paul is making to bring the faith to the church there. Further, the prize (βραβεῖον) alluded to in 2:16 is more forcefully spoken of in 3:12–14 and 4:1.[23] Paul's allusions to the stadium games are more than nuanced in 1 Corinthians 9:24–26. There he drew upon the games in Corinth to better illustrate to the believers in the city the life of the follower of Jesus.[24] Indeed, Anthony Thiselton suggests ἐν σταδίῳ could be translated as *stadium*, a choice that would transform the passage, moving it past the idea that Paul is merely speaking of a foot race, but quite possible the entirety of the arena games.[25] Hans Conzelmann adds to our understanding of Paul's metaphor by suggesting his self-designation (κηρύσσειν) is likely tied to the stadium as well.[26]

The sports metaphors emerge several more times in the Pauline corpus. In Galatians, the sports metaphor emerges twice (Gal 2:2; 5:7). This is followed by secondary Pauline literature, where the race is seen as surrounded by a cosmic arena (cf. Heb 12:1). The metaphor makes an appearance several times in the pastorals. In 1 Timothy 1:18 and 4:7–8, the training (for the race) prevents bad religion. In 2 Timothy 2:5 and 4:7, once again a prize emerges as the victor's crown, something the author of those letters would have us believe Paul is concerned with and demands the reader to focus on. Even with the earthly race in mind, each instance does have a cosmic focus, either with a heavenly audience (as in Heb 12:1) or with a heavenly gown (with the other references). However, these metaphors are usually limited to games, perhaps only requiring a symbolical sacrifice. The sacrifice, however, of the arena is a real one in several other references.

In 1 Corinthians 4:9, Paul is not necessarily bemoaning the spectacle, but rather places God as the one who puts the apostles on display in the

23. See Pfitzner, *Paul and the Agon Motif*, 139–41. Pfitzner demonstrates the oversaturation of athletic imagery in the Philippians passage.

24. Keener, *New Testament*, 1 Cor 9:24–25.

25. Thiselton, *First Corinthians*, 710.

26. Conzelmann, *1 Corinthians*, 163. Barratt disagrees; however, I favor Conzelmann here given that κηρύξας is used in connection with stadium. See Barrett, *First Epistle to the Corinthians*, 218.

arena.[27] In his mind, God has determined that the apostles are the gladiatorial show, the dénouement where one side will lose, suffer death, and be sacrificed. According to Conzelmann, Paul is adopting a Stoic stance in placing himself as the hero in a cosmic struggle. "The Stoic picture of the philosopher's struggle as a spectacle for the world is taken over by Paul into his world-picture (cosmos and angels) and reshaped in terms of his eschatology; 'spectacle' has for him a derogatory sense. He is thinking not of the warrior who is admired by God for his heroism, but of the scenes in the Roman theatre with those condemned to death."[28] It should not be surprising, then, to discover another such reference, perhaps even one causing more dread to the reader's mind, in Paul—and there is one in the same letter.

In 1 Corinthians 15:32, what began as an arena of games and moved to an gladiatorial combat, now emerges as a stadium of sacrifice—and it may be that Paul experienced the arena first hand.[29] As Keener notes, the victim of such sacrificial acts was not expected to survive, which is why the connection to the resurrection is important.[30] Likewise, this connection between the sacrifice in the arena and the resurrection provided by Christ is unambiguously found in 2 Corinthians 2:14–15. This idea that the spectacle is on a trajectory from a mere analogy of self-discipline in the life of the Christian to the emplotment of Paul's message is demonstrated in Colossians 2:14–15, where the author uses Pauline imagery to suggest that those who would usually be displayed at the games were the ones Jesus had freed from sacrifice by his sacrifice. More than that, those who had imprisoned the formerly bound were now led through the arena, ready to be sacrificed. The foes are better identified in Ephesians 6:12.

There can be no doubt that the audience reception of the Pauline corpus, even the disputed letters, included those familiar with the metaphor of sports and spectacle. Further, it would be wrong to single out the sports metaphor, stripping it away from the spectacle semiosis employed by Paul and subsequent writers. It was not merely an analogy of self-discipline, but encompassed the whole of the arena and as we see below, the spectacle. The use of it as an analogy includes human sacrifice, the cosmic audience,

27. Thiselton, *First Corinthians*, 359.

28. Conzelmann, *1 Corinthians*, 88–89.

29. See Thiselton, *First Corinthians*, 1252, for the discussion he seemingly hosts on the topic between the two opposing (literal v. hypothetical) views. For this study, it matters little, but I do side with the view that this is a metaphor.

30. Keener, *New Testament*, 1 Cor 15:32.

and even political suicide. That it is a prominent theme in the Pauline corpus only ensures Paul and his audience would have easily understood and accepted such semiotic endeavors, allowing us to better examine the role human sacrifice and the arena may have played in Galatia and the epistle bearing its name.

The spectacle remained a threat to the burgeoning Christian movement until the time of Eusebius. The ancient Christian rigorists, Tertullian in *de Spectaculis* and Novatian in a work by the same name, condemned the Spectacle as un-Christian, citing the pagan influences, idol worship, and even death by magical rites.[31] Further, they saw it as a battleground between God and the powers opposing God and his creation.[32] When the ritual gratification of the games waned due to the Christian triumph of Roman society, the stadiums, theaters, and arenas of the Empire shifted to leisurely pursuits, with gladiatorial combat shows becoming little more than chariot races even until the sixth century.[33]

Are the spectacle and the arena metaphors Paul employs important to Galatians? I tentatively argue yes, for the following reasons. As discussed above, Paul uses the games metaphor twice in the epistle (Gal 2:2; 5:7). Secondly, magical rites were used in the arena to subdue opponents, if not kill them. We find our author alluding to the possibility of his enemy's use of spells in 3:1 as well as in 5:20 to subdue the Galatians. If we understand Paul's use of κηρύσσειν as connected to the proclamation in the arena, then the portrayal he mentions (Gal 3:1) takes on a different light. In the vice list present in Galatians 5:19–21, the reader cannot help but notice the list of unvirtuous actions look eerily similar to that of the spectacle. Martyn has little trouble connecting the corruptions to certain deities mentioned above, such as Cybele. He also specifically ties εἰδωλολατρίαα to the former religious activities of the Galatians.[34] Unlike Betz who argues, that the vice list is nothing more than "a random collection of terms, describing the ordinary occurrences of evil among men," the list represents well the expected vices of the Spectacle, as it includes the issues of sensuality, local

---

31. Tertullian, *de Spect.*, 2.

32. Thomas Wiedemann argues Christian opposition to the games, notably beginning with Tertullian, is because the early Christians saw the games as a theological rivalry. See Wiedemann, *Emperors and Gladiators*, 1995.

33. Kyle, *Sport and Spectacle*, 334–35.

34. Martyn, *Galatians*, 496–97.

religion, and the dissension often times settled in the arena.[35] Finally, the entirety of the letter places Paul against adversaries, perhaps pitting the two opponents only in a rhetorical arena, but nevertheless they are fighting for the prize, that of the Galatians.[36]

A Bloody Spectacle in Galatia

Epictetus speaks of the madness attributed to the priests of Cybele.[37] This "madness" is nothing less than human sacrifice, albeit in an abbreviated form—an act Julius Caesar noticed among the same families of people in Gaul. From before Caesar to well after, historians noted this same peculiar ritual. The fourth-century Christian historian and bishop, Eusebius, recorded a long list of ancient cultures, some of which he knew, who regularly sacrificed humans as some form of ritual.[38] In this era, drunken initiates would practice self-induced castration (calling to mind Paul's hope in Gal 5:12). This was part of the stylized ritual associated with the various forms of a languishing Celtic religion.[39] One cannot hope to understand the role of Paul's imaging of the death (Gal 3:1) of Christ, nor the language of the offering of Christ (Gal 3:13–14) without first understanding the continuing role human sacrifice played in the life of the Galatian.

As mentioned above, during the time of Paul, hecatombs were offered as sacrifices—although, while they were not usually human in nature, they did involve blood, *symbolic* of a long-ago cultic sacrifice. They were "a mild and civilised representative of the Celtic and early Galatian custom of human sacrifices on a gigantic scale."[40] This devolved from the use of captives as sacrifices.[41] Of course, we must note the hecatombs were blood sacrifices

35. Betz, *Galatians*, 283. See also Longenecker, *Galatians*, 254, who agrees with him.

36. I cannot fail to mention the use of sports and political metaphors in 4 Maccabees. In chapter 3, I will discuss Paul's use of Maccabean martyrology while below I address Stoicism as part of Paul's cognitive environment. For the connection of these three areas, see Moore and Anderson, "Taking It Like a Man," 249–73; Pfitzner, *Paul and the Agon Motif*, 58; Renehan, "Greek Philosophic Background," 223–38.

37. Epictetus, *Disc.* 2.20.17.

38. Eusebius, *Theophania*, 2.53–64.

39. Harrill, "Asia Minor," 134–135.

40. Ramsay, *Galatians*, 133.

41. Ramsey, *Historical Commentary*, 78. The Irish Celts would still practice human sacrifice, however, only finding its end when Christianity became established. See Snyder, *Irish Jesus, Roman Jesus*.

in other relevant cultures, including the Hellenistic, as is the case demonstrated in Homer's picture of the gods "feasting on hecatombs."[42] We find a similar sacrifice in Virgil's *Aeneid* as well.[43] Finally, the Sibylline Oracles were not estranged from the use of hecatombs in appeasing, albeit a familiar one, God.[44] Eusebius allows for the connection of the hecatombs and human sacrifice.[45]

However, beyond that we have a significant contribution to the knowledge of ritual human sacrifice in the *koinon* of Galatia. Accounts beginning forty years before the birth of Jesus have the local ruler, Castor Tarcondarius (who had supported Pompey and Cato at Pharsalus), beginning the long line of offering official hecatombs as well as human sacrifice in the form of gladiatorial combat.[46] He was not the last, as Pylamenes (son of Amyntos) likewise sacrificed a hecatomb combined with bouts of physical strength. Gallios and Pylaimenes, who both offered the human sacrifice of the gladiatorial games mixed with the sacrifice of hecatombs, followed in this line.[47]

The exaggerated role of the gladiatorial arena and the games it housed is not to be dismissed. Not only does it serve a significant role in Roman ritual, but also was very likely the center of city life. Combat in these arenas were often mimetic performances of cosmic struggle. It allowed groups to act in recreating foundational myths, with one faction winning in a way so as to honor the gods of the community. Actual victory was not something that concerned the group, nor a true-to-life method: what mattered was the blood spilled in the arena for the gods. Indeed, combat was central to Celtic life as noted by numerous Roman historiographers of the time. As Futrell points out, the Celtic diaspora used these games as "intertribal exchanges" even with their neighbors. What the arena did was to placate any notion of tribal blood lust by allowing a regular sacrifice, ritualizing feasts and even

---

42. Homer, *Iliad*, 9.535.

43. Virgil, *Aeneid*, 5.509.

44. *Sib. Or.* 3.625–628.

45. Eusebius, *Theoph.* 2.69.

46. The Celtic inhabits of the Greco-Roman area were not the first to do this. John Mouratidis believes that the rise of gladiatorial games in the Greek world began as a direct result of cultural memory of human sacrifice. From the Greeks, the Romans picked it up, complete with the same cultural memory edifices. See his article, Mouratidis, "On the Origin," 111–34.

47. Jones and Ehrenberg, *Documents Illustrating the Reigns*.

transfer of tribal leadership.[48] These Gauls were memorialized at the Great Altar of Pergamum.

Just as the arena was important for the Celts across their diaspora, Rome too shared a place for it. While we are tempted to see the arena as a lavish spectacle, Futrell reminds us that it was not as simple as that. She draws a comparison between the imperial arena (we cannot forget that the arena, Celtic in origin, nevertheless rested on Roman lands) and other cultures. She is able to then propose, "the amphitheater was a politicized temple that housed the mythic reenactment of the cult of Roman statehood."[49] This ongoing myth validated Rome's power and authority, even in lands that resisted assimilation. It was, even in the colonized provinces, a society of the spectacle.

One such case is the mysterious scene of *arae Perusinae*. The surrender of the town is captured in Appian's *Civil War*,[50] the poet Sextus Propertius, and by other Roman authors. It records a rather terrible event by Octavian, who upon winning the victory took it upon himself to sacrifice three hundred warriors as a way to cement the peace accord. In a scene echoed throughout history, pleas are made to the conquering General who simply responds, "You must die."[51] The three hundred were led to an altar consecrated to *divus Iulius*, specifically on the Ides of March, and ritually slaughtered in accordance with ancient Roman ritual to appease the deceased Julius.[52]

Beyond the sheer brutality of the arena is the use of the arena for political manipulation. In Rome, the arena was not only the place chosen to honor Pompey, but also the place where Caesar was murdered. Likewise, it would sometimes host the Senate and funerals, such as the dramatic showing of Caesar's body.[53] There was no end to the use of it as a symbol of political power and pageantry, connecting all of the ancient Roman religions—deity, state, and leisure—into one geographical locale. Indeed, Octavian would rebuild the Roman forum, but include in it the dedicated

---

48. Futrell, *Blood in the Arena*, 106–10.

49. Futrell, *Blood in the Arena*, 170.

50. Appian, *B. Civ.* 5.cc.48.

51. Seutonius, *Augustus*, 15.

52. Frothingham, "Propertius and the Arae Perusinae," 345–352. See also Reid, "Human Sacrifices," 42–43. This is not the only time 300 (or so) were sacrificed. The Tarquinians (c. 358 BCE) sacrificed 307 Romans (Livy 7.15–19). The infamous Spartacus (c. 72 BCE) likewise sacrificed 300 Romans (Appian, *B. Civ.* 1.117).

53. Beacham, *Spectacle Entertainment*, 88–91.

temple to *Divus Iulius* among other temples, all built with a new priesthood dedicated to religious revival. This was not merely a chance refurbishment, but a ritual reenacted across the empire so that the arena continuously held religious meaning.[54]

Kathleen Coleman's work reveals the arena as a place of mythological reenactment via death.[55] This "mitigated death penalty" is given new life in the Roman amphitheater where Greek tragedies were reenacted along with mythological slaughters of prisoners of war or others in need of the Roman's particular view of justice. In at least one instance, one participant, in reenacting the death of Laurelous was actually crucified, an act forever memorialized by a line (*non falsa penens in cruce*) in Martial's Epigram. Likewise, the death of Jesus was recreated time and time again, according to both record and legend (specifically, Peter's infamous death on the upside down cross). In one instance, a third-century Christian by the name of Ardalion was portrayed as being publicly crucified before an expecting audience, but was ultimately denied the honorific death.[56] Finally, in this game, is the appearance of the sacrificial victim who often times wore the clothing of a priest.[57]

While I will cover more fully the use of sacrifice in the political life of Rome and specifically, Roman Anatolia, in the next chapter, what must be noted is the use of the arena, including the expectations of the audience. Coleman's work goes a long way in proving that by just a few turn of phrases, key images, or a bare allusion, the audience would recognize the myth playing out in front of them. Further, as noted throughout this section, the use of death before the audience was not simply perfunctory; but usually carried with it some deeper significance related to statecraft.

---

54. It is unwise to separate the activities in the city of Rome from the activities in provinces, especially in Anatolia. With Augustus's ascent, tight Roman control over Anatolia increased. This also increased and changed the role of the gladiatorial games. See Ramsay, "Studies in the Roman Province Galatia," 229–83; Mitchell, *Anatolia*, 112–17.

55. Coleman, "Fatal Charades," 44–73.

56. Migne, *Patrologia Graeca* 117.407.

57. Colemon, "Fatal Charades," 66. For more on "fatal charades" and how this system of entertainment merged justice, religion, and entertain systems, see Monaghan, "Bloody Roman Narratives"; Levinson, "Tragedies Naturally Performed."

STOICISM

In this section, I will explore the role of Stoicism in Paul's world and the audiential domain as well as evidence of Stoicism in Galatians. Much like the spectacle and sacrifice, Stoicism provides definition to Paul's model of the death of Jesus including the cosmological outcome of this event. This aural trifecta provides the precipitants of Paul's letter, both Jewish and Gentile, an understanding of Paul's message that will be explored in the remainder of this study. I will briefly detail cosmology and anthropology (specifically, freedom of the will) in Stoicism and then turn to Stoicism in the region of the epistle's reception and Stoicism in Paul.[58] The possible divine status of a human will be covered in chapter 4, as it is too tied to *devotio* to too easily separate. What will emerge is a foundation for understanding the role of self-sacrifice in cosmological struggles as well as how this serves as an impetus for understanding the death of Jesus as *devotio*.

Far from the mundane emotionless and ethic-centered image of Stoics vulcanized in our minds, the Stoics had a profound view on a range of subjects, from proper emotions to the gods. In regards to the latter, the dialogue between other theologies of the time presents a divine actor with intent to care for the cosmos he created.[59] The deity even participates in ordering fate, providing for certain times and events in the course of the cosmos.[60] The Stoic cosmos was sustained by an equal-with-god *pneuma*, bringing about various points in history.[61] For Stoics of the time, their deity could easily be seen as *fictricem et moderatricem*,[62] and one who was always active, even in the times of the conflagration. However, a later Stoic poet, Lucan, while seeing the gods as active, could just as easily see the gods as nihilistic performers, somewhat removed from—and as a result of their removal, the cause of—the conflagration.[63] It may be a better application of Stoicism to understand the time periods in which an author wrote. Cicero was writing at the birth of the Empire, while Lucan was lamenting the rise of Nero and the existence of the Empire. Regardless, the deity, or deities, of

---

58. Ethics, theology, and cosmology are all tied together in Stoicism. See Thorsteinsson, *Roman Christianity and Roman Stoicism*, 32.

59. See Thomas Bénatouïl's essay, Bénatouïl, "How Industrious can Zeus be."

60. Bobzien, *Determinism and Freedom*, 45–53.

61. Salles, *Stoics on Determinism and Compatibilism*, 63–66.

62. Cicero, *De Natura Deorum* 3.92.

63. Lucan, *Civil War*, xxii.

Stoicism allows for a cosmos that is a concern for a divine actor, and such concern is related to the conflagration and cosmogony.[64]

In regards to the conflagration, the cyclical renewal of the cosmos through fire, Salles writes, "The conflagration thereby involves the elimination of any differentiation. Thus, in order for this elimination to occur, the sustaining cause of the world, or god, must stop its activity *qua* sustaining cause of the world."[65] Aune notes, "Stoicism taught a periodic conflagration *(ekpyrosis)* and reconstitution *(palingenesia)*. . . . The Stoics even spoke of these cosmic cycles in terms of the beginning *(arche)* and end *(telos)* and of significant events which changed the character of the world."[66] Not all Stoics accepted this lack of divine activity during and immediately after the conflagration, but it does give us a connection to the cosmology of Galatians, which we will explore later. A portion of Stoic thought, then, involves an active deity that is at best inactive during the conflagration, a time of crisis ending in a renewal of the cosmos.[67] Further, the *pneuma* of the cosmos, identified with the deity, moves history along to each conflagration according to certain designated plot points.

This study will use two aspects of Stoic anthropology to examine Paul's presentation of the death of Jesus—free will and the deification, or divinization, of a person. As stated above, the latter aspect will find a natural place for examination in the chapter on *devotio*. However, the road to the *devotio* is found in the cosmological struggles exemplified by Stoicism; the divine nature of the victim is as well; however, what is lacking thus far is the will of the victim, something likewise understood via Stoicism and its influence on Hellenistic Judaism. As we will discover in chapter 4, the freedom of the victims will become an indispensable emplotment of the overall story. The victim must have freedom of will because the ransom offered *must* be self-sacrifice. What follows is a brief review of this aspect, specifically in regards to the agency of the person in self-inflicted death, of Stoicism's anthropology.

It is rather anachronistic to style the debate within Stoic orthodoxy as "free will versus determinism." Frede notes that the Stoics would have

---

64. See also Brunt et al., *Studies in Stoicism*, 492–94.

65. Salles, *Stoics on Determinism and Compatibilism*, 67.

66. Aune, "Eschatology," 598.

67. See Trompf, *Idea of Historical Recurrence*, 8–10. Tromphf details the act of conflagration, a cosmological concern wherein the world would be renewed or transformed.

avoided such terminology given the political conations of "freedom."[68] Determinism, as Meyer reminds us, is not fatalism, although Stoics are often accused of the latter.[69] The more palatable, and modern, term in describing the stance of the Stoics is compatibilism, with such a paradoxical take grounded in the Stoic notion of *pneuma*.[70]

In regards to death, rather than the annihilationism of the Epicureans, the Stoics viewed death as the best of all states of existence.[71] Pabst Battin sees this as an encouragement for suicide, something he also finds in Christianity.[72] However, early challenges to the notion that Stoic works encouraged suicide, such as Plato's *Phaedo*, exist. Cicero[73] casually recalls an epigram wherein a reader of the work kills himself. Augustine recounts the story,[74] but includes as admonition that Plato, the author of the work, did not kill himself. This for the theologian serves as a prohibition against taking one's life. James Warren has issued a modern call on reexamined *Phaedo*, suggesting that the work is written in such a way as to speak against self-killing.[75]

It may be that Augustine was drawing on Cicero to understand Plato who rails against self-killing. In *De Republica* 6.15, Cicero writes of the god who has a temple of the cosmos, and as such is the one to whom the soul and life belongs. It is then the duty of Publius and all of those who venerate the gods to preserve "the wonderful union of body and soul" and to avoid "quitting life."

Further,

> But Cato left this world in such a manner as if he were delighted that he had found an opportunity of dying; for that god who presides in us forbids our departure hence without his permission. But when god himself has given us a just cause, as formerly he did to Socrates, and lately to Cato, and often to many others—in such a case, certainly every man of sense would gladly exchange this

68. Frede, "Stoic Determinism," 179–205.

69. Meyer, "Fate, Fatalism, and Agency."

70. Frede, "Stoic Determinism," 192

71. Cicero's defense of Stoicism in regards to self-killing is often set against Epicurean statements, so that the morality of self-killing takes on a larger role, such as ethics, determinism, and the after life. See Hill, *Ambitiosa Mors*, 33–35.

72. Battin, *Ethics of Suicide*, 29, 64–65.

73. Cicero, *Tus. Dis.* 1.84.

74. Augustine, *Civ. Dei* 1.22.

75. Warren, "Socratic Suicide," 91–106.

darkness for that light: not that he would forcibly break from the chains that held him, for that would be against the law; but, like a man released from prison by a magistrate or some lawful authority, so he too would walk away, being released and discharged by God. For the whole life of a philosopher is, as the same philosopher says, a meditation on death.[76]

While Plato may have been misunderstood, Seneca's *Ep.* 70 is not.[77] In this epistle, along with *Ep.* 77, Seneca gives the most detailed view of self-killing from the Stoic perspective near the time of Paul, but in regards to Stoicism as a whole around the time, Seneca provides us a rather remarkable window. In regards to determinism, Seneca follows the normative understanding of a first cause and two principles of the nature of things[78]; however, Seneca goes further, suggesting that by some sacrifice (expiation), the determined outcome may be averted.[79] He objects to the use of expiation and propitiation ceremonies to change Fate's ultimate course; however, there is room to bring about incremental changes because those deviations are designed by Fate.[80]

Let me briefly return to *Ep.* 70 in order to note for the purposes of this study, Seneca relies heavily on the image of the spectacle to influence his reader's perception. The philosopher contrasts the games, and the resolve of the participants in facing death, with other literary voices, such as Telesphorus of Rhodes. Telesphorus uttered the phrase, *modo liceat vivere, est spes*, which caused Seneca to berate the speaker's manhood.[81] For Seneca, self-killing is directly connected to determinism—because it is the ultimate act of liberty.[82] The two views, that Fate does accept sacrifices but only sacrifices it has designed, and that self-killing is ultimate liberty against Fate, must be contrasted.

---

76. Cicero, *Tusculan Disputations* 1.74–5.

77. Evenpoel, "Philosopher Seneca on Suicide," 217–43.

78. Seneca, *Ep.* 65.2–4.

79. Cicero notes that Chrysippus, Antipater, and Posidonius understood the use of sacrifices as one in which the victim was chosen by the deity (Cicero, *Div.* 2.35).

80. Seneca, *Nat. quaest.* 2.38.3 Inwood, "God and Human Knowledge" 40–41.

81. See Cicero, *Ad Att.* 9.10.3.

82. Seneca, *Ep.* 70.24. According to Anton J. L. Van Hooff, Seneca and his nephew Lucan's suicide should be understood as a rebellion against political tyranny, which is why the suicides took on a heroic form, and thus remained palatable to Stoics. See Van Hooff, *From Autothanasia to Suicide.*

Between Plato and Seneca, there was a change in the acceptance of self-killing. Rather than the revolution occurring because of some moral decline, shift in public philosophy, or even a necessity to curb population, the ultimate reason suicide became an acceptable form of death in the Empire is exactly because of one man, the hidden focus of this present study—Cato the Younger, the Stoic legend. Before Cato, autothanasia was usually limited to women who had suffered sexual humiliation and men who had lost honor on the battlefield.[83] However, after Cato's death, suicide took a rather trend-setting turn perhaps in part due to the literary works devoted to the deceased general. His life was seen as one to be imitated, and his death quickly achieved the same status, a status employed by Brutus and Cassius. Further, because Augustus limited imperial honors to members of his family, citizens found other ways to be remembered, turning to imitation of Cato's death. The death of aristocrats would often mimic the tale of Cato versus Julius Caesar.[84] The action of Cato, a person who embodied Stoic ideals, changed the philosophy's understanding of suicide, which would later enable Seneca and other Stoics to see the act quite differently than their forbearers.[85]

Given Cicero's reaction against self-killing as a rather anti-Stoic thing to do, because it takes on the role of determining Fate (the realm of the deity), it is surprising his accept of Cato's death.

> Indeed, such diversity of character carries with it so great significance that suicide may be for one man a duty, for another [under the same circumstances] a crime. Did Marcus Cato find himself in one predicament, and were the others, who surrendered to Caesar in Africa, in another? And yet, perhaps, they would have been condemned, if they had taken their lives; for their mode of life had been less austere and their characters more pliable. But Cato had been endowed by nature with an austerity beyond belief, and he himself had strengthened it by unswerving consistency and had remained ever true to his purpose and fixed resolve; and it was for him to die rather than to look upon the face of a tyrant.[86]

83. Van Hooff, *From Autothanasia to Suicide*, 50.

84. Van Hooff, *From Autothanasia to Suicide*, 109.

85. For a fuller discussion on the role Cato's suicide played in changing the Roman use of suicide, see Farrior, "Ultimate Romana Mors."

86. Cicero, *De Officiis*, 115.

What may be seen in this brief examination of Stoic anthropology is that suicide and determinism are interwoven. The Stoics had what can be best understood as a compatibilist understanding of the will—best demonstrated in Cicero's aversion to suicide and Seneca's acceptance of it. Fate is set, but it can be changed—although Stoic orthodox had differing opinions as to agency and how much change could actually happen. Change itself is connected to liberty and freedom of the deity and the human. Morality is at play and prayer does sometimes work. Finally, as with Cato, a single death may in fact change perceptions on certain reactions, such as Cato's death to suicide and the death of Jesus to martyrdom.

Stoicism in Galatians

The New Testament flirts with Stoicism, whether it is the pastorals and their use of Plutarch or the Book of Acts and its direct mentioning of Stoicism along a Stoic celebrity, the early Jesus movement—like other Jewish groups—used Stoicism, sometimes as a foil, sometimes as recruiting ground, and sometimes as theological fodder.[87] In regards to the Book of Acts, this is perhaps our clearest statement on Paul's appeal and use of Stoicism in expanding his early *kerygma*.

In Acts 17:18, 22–29, the author mentions two schools of Greek thought—the Epicureans and the Stoics. The former is dismissed out of hand, because it is the Stoics Paul is after.[88] As Craig Keener notes, several of the phrases the author uses is meant to cast Paul in the light of other famous Stoics, such as Socrates.[89] Why? Because the Stoics had common ground with the Jewish believers in Jesus such as the existence of deities that do not need a temple or physical comforts, a shared understanding of divine boundaries, and the immortality of the soul.[90] But, Paul was not alone in connecting his cognitions to the Stoics, as a writer before him (Philo) and another after him (Josephus) would often find common ground

87. Betz, *Plutarch's Theological Writings*, 1975.

88. The Epicureans would find no favor in later Christian writings, as Lactantius (late third century), still derided them in his writings.

89. Gorman, *Apostle of the Crucified Lord*, 86, cites other phrases Paul gleaned from the Stoics.

90. Keener, *New Testament*, Acts 17:18, 21–31. For more on Paul's attempted syncretism with Stoicism in this passage, see also Conzelmann, *Acts of the Apostles*, 139; Pervo, *Acts*, 430–31; Barrett, *Acts of the Apostles*, 829; Squires, "Acts," 1249.

with the Greeks.[91] As to Paul's familiarity with the Stoics, it may be due to the place of his birth, Tarsus, where a Stoic school known for the remarkable contributions of its students remained for centuries.[92]

Admittedly, much of my proposal for Paul's use of *devotio* as a model for the death of Jesus is reliant upon an allowance of Stoicism and more notably, the role of Cato the Younger in making suicide a part of Stoicism. The school of thought helps to explain the cosmological struggles propelling Paul's Jesus to voluntarily offer himself as a sacrifice, what this freedom of will means about Jesus, and how such an event could actually recreate a new world, or dispensation of the old. Stoicism, specifically a Stoicism of post-Republican and early-Imperial Rome, helps to better understand the central role Jesus' death will take in Galatians. Because of this, it is necessary to outline a few of the Stoic features of the Epistle to the Galatians, as these connections give us a ground to look further for a Stoic setting, or appeal as we saw in Acts. Because they exist, then the use of the *devotio* is allowable.

In Troels Engberg-Pedersen's volume, Galatians ranks behind Romans for the Pauline epistle with the most references to Stoicism.[93] Beyond the virtue/vice list explored above, there are key themes in Galatians that share something with Stoicism—such as freedom, elements, and the unity of humanity.[94] It may as well be that Paul even learned his style of discourse from the Stoics.[95] In order to maintain the precept that Galatians' best rendering is within a Stoic framework, rather than going into a full examination of the epistle, I will present only a brief argument. I will focus on the above-mentioned categories, specifically Galatians 3:26–29; 4:3, 8–10, and the concept of ἐλευθερία in Galatians 5.

Galatians 3:26–29 expresses Paul's eschatological hope in the unity of humanity, much as he does with other references to the "body of Christ."[96]

---

91. For an introduction to Philo's Stoicism, see Horsley, "Law of Nature"; Graver, "Philo of Alexandria." Johnson notes that Josephus designs his schools of Jewish thought along the lines of Greek schools, with the Pharisees taking the place of the Stoics (Johnson, *Among the Gentiles*, 123), which cannot be an accident.

92. Sedley, "School," 30–31.

93. Engberg-Pedersen, *Paul and the Stoics*, 2000.

94. For the earliest compounding of the various lists, see Vögtle, *Die Tugend und Lasterkataloge*. Recent lists, and a thorough discussion of the lists and Stoicism, can be found in Fitzgerald, "Virtue/Vice Lists," 857.

95. Dunn, *Galatians*, 329.

96. This passage must be compared to Paul's speech to the Stoics in Acts 17:26–28,

This is not a new approach to this concept, as we find it in Cicero, Seneca, and other Stoic philosophers.[97] Moreover, this passage, if it is an early baptismal formula, may have an origin in Stoicism.[98] What Paul and the Stoics both shared is a "belief in the common humanity of all men, irrespective of their status" and a seeming inconsistency in challenging the natural order over such things as slavery, although both found common humanity with the slave.[99] Epictetus, a late contemporary of Paul, would in his writings explicitly charge his Stoic followers to remember the slave as of the same offspring of God.[100] A bare reading of Paul's words here reveals an eschatological hope of absolute unity in humanity, based on our commonality; however, like the Stoics, Paul has no need to force the implementation now.[101] In fact, for Paul it is only *in Christ* where this ultimate unity can take place—a move past the Stoics.[102]

Our second passage (Gal 4:3, 8–10) deals with a favorite Stoic theme—the end of the controlling forces. DeMaris outlines several possible interpretations of the elements: celestial bodies connected to worship; demons or spirits controlling human destiny; or, the four "constituents of the universe." He writes,

> By ascribing enslaving power to the elements (Gal 4:3, 9), Paul understands them to be active cosmic forces, which was the contemporary understanding of the four elements. Philo, for example, regarded the four elements as forces (*dynameis*; Aet 21.107–8), while the early Christian writer Hermas noted that they governed the world (*Herm. Vis.* 3.13.3). Paul's placement of the four elements among the powers of the present age led him to view them in a negative light.[103]

---

where Paul quotes a Stoic poet.

97. See Lee, *Paul*, for a full discussion on Paul's use of the metaphor of "body" and its connection to the Stoics. The metaphor does not appear easily Galatians, although the concept of common humanity is easily seen in Galatians 3:26–29.

98. Martyn, *Galatians*, 379.

99. Brunt, *Studies in Stoicism*, 298. See also, Thorsteinsson, *Roman Christianity and Roman Stoicism*, 31–32.

100. Epictetus, *Diss* 1.13.3–4. Peter Oakes notes the value of Epictetus in reading Paul (Oakes, "Epictetus," 39–56).

101. See Cicero, *Fin.* 3.19.63

102. As Ernest Best notes, the language in this passage does not include a physical body. See Best, *One Body in Christ*.

103. DeMaris, "Element, Elemental Spirit," 444–45.

This, if not directly connected to Stoic thought, offers a resemblance of Stoic physics that is too coincidental to be accidental. In Galatians 4.6, the connection becomes clear as Paul contrasts the elements with the Spirit, something the ancient Stoic would have recognized as well. White remarks for the ancient Stoic, "*pneuma* seems often to function in much the way that the active principle (creative fire or god) does—whereas its ontological status appears to be not even that of an element, but rather a synthesis of elements."[104] Eduard Schweizer, after an examination of the continued use of the elements in Paul and Deutero-Pauline, concludes "this power was probably also feared by the Galatians, though the Jewish influence was certainly stronger there. Worshiped were, on the contrary, those 'angels' or 'saviors' or 'beings that are by nature no gods' that were believed to help the soul in its ascent to heaven."[105] Paul, coopting Stoic cosmology, contrasts the enslavement of the soul to the elements, a situation that gave no real hope for the individual, with the freedom found in the Spirit.

It is to this concept, ἐλευθερία, we now turn, especially exhibited in the final two chapters of the epistle. Galatians 5 begins with a pointed statement, "It is with liberty that Christ has liberated his people."[106] Recall our earlier discussions on the freedom of the will. Paul is enforcing the idea to the readers that by Jesus' own freedom of will he has liberated those now placed in him (by baptism), which then brings to light new responsibilities.[107] The death of Jesus also brings them new possibilities, possibilities (such as escaping the conflagration) that are impossible under the Law (and the elemental forces of the world).[108] Further, the whole of freedom is connected back to the common unity of humanity, in that our identity in Jesus is simultaneous to our behavior, so that our freedom affects our behavior.[109] We are given a new identity, and thus a new behavior—or, as Paul would say, a new rule (Gal 6:15–16).[110]

---

104. White, "Stoic Natural Philosophy," 134–35.

105. Schweizer, "Slaves of the Elements," 468.

106. Bruce, *Galatians*, 226.

107. See Frede, "Stoic Determinism," 200–1.

108. See Engberg-Pedersen, "Stoicism in the Apostle Paul."

109. Engberg-Pedersen, *Paul and the Stoics*, 326–27.

110. In Gal 6:16, Paul uses κανών in the same Stoics such as Chrysippus and Senaca would (See Inwood, "Rules and Reasoning," 116–17). This is to be read next to Paul's use of a familiar term in Gal 5:16 (Keener, *New Testament*, Gal 6:16).

CONCLUSION

To properly read Galatians, we have to have been in the first audience and to be attuned to Paul's rhetorical skill. At best, second—and later—generation readers must first discover the original audience and determine what mattered to them in listening, and then decide if Paul found those things suitable to his needed narrative. I have chosen to follow Martyn and others in seeing the letter written to, rather than a geographical locale, people of Celtic descent. Likewise, because of the confrontational first century BCE, these peoples who were first Hellenized and then Romanized, could offer Paul the allowance of including various Roman elements into his history. Galatians must be read in light of a heavily Romanized Celtic diaspora that utilized the divinization of the arena and contains a universe animated by Stoic philosophy. In this reading light, we can then better read Paul's use of vows, devotions, and freedom—as well as, as noted above, the lists of vices and virtues.

Chapter 3

Self-Inflicted Death among Jewish Sources

INTRODUCTION

A NOBLE BUT SELF-CHOSEN death is thought of as almost a uniquely Roman attribute;[1] yet there are several examples found in the Jewish scriptures of people ending their own lives by choice and without judgment. The act of martyrdom is usually attributed to early Christians as an act featured prominently in the Gospels as a mark promised by Jesus to his disciples. Between these two not-so-distant worlds, the Jews not only experienced death by self-infliction and self-choice, but created specific theological concepts to preserve innocence for the victim as well as set boundaries for what was and what was not acceptable, including suicide. This chapter will examine in detail beliefs surrounding the self-inflicted and self-chosen death in Jewish thought relevant to the time.[2]

---

1. See the conclusion to this section. The refusal to see a beneficial death in Jewish theology of the time would only allow the interpreter a position that Gentile Christians added a violent atonement to the Jesus movement. This action dismisses the very Jewish beginning of the Jewish movement as well as the very real Jewish Jesus.

2. Throughout this chapter, I attempt to differentiate between "self-inflicted" and "self-chosen." Self-inflicted is what we might call a suicide, whereas self-chosen is the victim, usually without premeditation, choosing to die such as a noble death or martyrdom.

Where as some may see a separation of categories, the lines are usually seen as too fine to separately classify.[3] Throughout this chapter, I hope to present a separation of these terms based not on the manner of the death, but on the victim's intent.[4] In a larger sense, the presentation of this chapter is not to establish any new theories, but only to insure that the death of Jesus, intentionally and methodically taken by his own hand as it were, was well within cognitive expectations and allowances available to the audience of Paul's letter. I also hope to show the death of Jesus does not fit easily into the categories of noble death or martyrdom.

3. Suicide is usually defined in Western society as the taking of one's life. However, recent philosophical discussions have removed this usual normative proscription in defining suicide. See Frey, "Suicide and Self-Inflicted Death," 193–202; Windt, "Concept of Suicide," 76. Individually, they allow suicide is now a rather inclusive term for those who purposely kill themselves—as well as those who have themselves killed or allow themselves to be killed. Frey does not allow the term "self-inflicted" to be used, however, if the person has established a way to avoid having to kill him or herself. This is a rather narrow view of self-infliction, and while Frey is generally correct, I disagree with him on this point. See also Holland, "Suicide," 143–57, esp. 151n8. However, Michael Wreen offers the definition of suicide that is necessary in erasing the lines between categories such as suicide and martyrdom. He writes, "A person commits suicide at time (*t*) if and only if (1) the person strongly intends to kill himself (or strongly wants to let himself die) at *t*; (2) the person killed himself at *t*; (3) the intention in (1) caused (2) via the intermediary of a number of generated actions; (4) the causal route from (1) to (2) was more or less in accord with his action plan; and (5) the person acted voluntarily in killing himself" (Wreen cited in Donnelly, *Suicide*, 30n7). Emile Durkheim sees suicide as a "death resulting directly or indirectly from a positive or negative act of the victim himself which he knows will product this result" (Durkheim, *Suicide*, 44). While Robert L. Barry (see chapter 1) wished to present a definition of suicide that was open enough to prevent historic Catholic condemnation of the act but closed enough to prevent the death of Jesus as understand as suicide, his definition is the one I will use in this work to suggest Paul's image of Jesus—if not the image of Jesus found in the New Testament—is that of a Jesus who deliberately sought his own death. He writes, "A suicide is a deliberate and voluntary performance or omission, done with adequate freedom and knowledge, that aims at the destruction of one's life. It is a planned, chosen, intended, and consented action to bring death as either a means or an end in itself. It is a choice made where death is reasonably expected to result from the specified performance or omission in common circumstances and situations" (Barry, *Thread of Life*, 10). We must add to that that "self-inflicted" is not limited to physical actions by the person, but can simply be the intellectual choice to force and then allow one's death. Margaret Pabst Battin has abandoned the search for nuance, replacing it with an inquiry into the morality of it. See Battin, *Ethical Issues in Suicide*, 21–22.

4. I maintain suicide, if the definition were broad enough, would encompass many stories of martyrdom.

This examination will deviate into two separate categories. The first part will examine Jewish views of self-inflicted death, notably those views usually defined as self-chosen death and martyrdom. There is a difference between self-inflicted death and martyrdom, notably the intention to refuse to commit blasphemy; therefore, one could take their own life (or presumably the life of an innocent) if it meant that religious desecration would not occur.[5] This would have been a form of martyrdom rather than, as we will see, the self-chosen noble death. The second part will survey human sacrifice in the same thought-world. Both are united at the basic level of taking a human life, although the first type includes taking or giving one's own life freely while the second does not necessarily include free will but does not exclude it either.[6] The Roman concept of *devotio* does not fit easily into these categories as understood by the Jews, although it does involve taking or offering one's own life as a sacrifice to appease or satisfy a deity due to cosmological distresses—although we do find at least one Jewish example comes strikingly close. Thus, while it is a self-inflicted death, it fits the definition of human sacrifice. The final portion of this chapter will examine the rabbinic reactions to voluntary death, especially where those reactions include the language of self-sacrifice. I do this, at length, to show that a premeditated and self-death of Jesus would not have been out of the realm of Jewish acceptable practice.

Self-Inflicted Death

While modern Jewish and Christian prohibitions against suicide are usually thought to be grounded in biblical tradition, the allowance of causing one's own death is expressed by various Jewish sources, including what is now called the New Testament. The Hebrew canon is replete with suicides, with the number of those deaths varying. While the Greco-Roman model provides for us certain ritualistic expectations and rules, as well as help in formulating later Christian theology, we can only gain from the Jewish world that the history of suicide in Jewish writings before the Rabbinic age lacked condemnation—and that at least in one instance, suicide involved

5. The separation only comes if we narrow the definition of suicide. See Goldstein, *Suicide in Rabbinic Literature*, 41–47.

6. The need for the death to be freely chosen is important to this current work. This aspect of choice will be explored throughout this chapter.

legendary praise for the action.[7] Even then, Rabbis (see below) while out-right condemning suicide, made many allowances for similarly looking actions. Due to this lack of cultic rituals for self-inflicted death, I can only use examples of Jewish suicides as a way to hypothesize that self-inflicted deaths were not only known to the Jews, but were also appreciated under certain conditions.[8] Thus, I will identify several examples from Jewish writings (canonical and non-canonical) to make this illustration. The case will be examined to present the cause, either internal or external; the manner, by which I mean either physically self-inflicted or planned to allow some-one else to do it; and the intent, if any.

Judges 9 tells the story of a would-be king. In the pericope, a descen-dent of Gideon, Abimelech, began his reign by hiring an army of mer-cenaries, slaying his seventy brothers, and assumed kingship over Israel. His reign lasted only three years until the God of Israel began to remind the people of Abimelech's crimes (a divine interaction). A short civil war ensued, a war wherein Abimelech laid waste to the city of Shechem, first besieging it, finally capturing it, only to then kill all of the inhabitants and salt the land.[9] He attempted to do the same to the town of Thebez, but was thwarted when he sought to massacre the inhabitants of the town who had retreated into a small fortress at the center of town. Abimelech suffered injury when a woman threw a millstone at him, fracturing his skull, leaving him helpless to do anything but speak (Judg 9:54–57).

His death was meant to preserve his honor and image, but from the angle of the audience, it was used as a payment for the sins he had commit-ted. While he was injured and likely to die, the fault of his death lies upon

---

7. Because the mentions of suicide were not accompanied with mentions of either condemnation or penalty, David Daube has suggested suicide is best seen as either natu-ral or perhaps even heroic. See Daube, "Death as a Release," 82–104. See also Bloch and Heyd, "Suicide," 232.

8. Suicide was common enough, at least in the time of Josephus, to have ritualistic responses, but not ritualistic manners of how to do so. See *BJ* 3.372–77, where Josephus notes that the bodies of suicide victims were left out in the sun and simply buried be-cause of the great crime they had committed against God. Their souls were sent to divine punishment.

9. See below for the use of such tactics as a form of *devotio*. Unlike the Roman con-quest of Carthage, Shechem's fall does not contain obvious elements of a ritual. However, several have noted the unique situation presented in Shechem. There is clearly a cosmo-logical struggle between Baal and El (YHWH is notably absent). The towers that serve as the final holdout of the town's people are temples (Zertal, "Shechem," 1187). Finally, there is the use of salting of the land, which is usually a part of a curse (Matthews et al., *IVP Bible*, Judg 9:45; Block, *Judges, Ruth*, 330).

himself. He required his armor-bearer to take his life so that his warrior status could be preserved. Unlike many of the following examples, we hear nothing of his burial or the reaction (mourning) to his passing. He simply vanishes from the text.

There are two suicides in 1 Samuel 31:4–5,

> The Philistines engaged Israel in battle, and the Israelites were routed, leaving their dead on Mount Gilboa. The Philistines closely pursued Saul and his sons, and Jonathan, Abinadab, and Malchishua, the sons of Saul, were killed. The battle went hard for Saul, and when the archers caught up with him they wounded him severely. He said to his armour-bearer, 'Draw your sword and run me through, so that these uncircumcised brutes may not come and taunt me and make sport of me.' But the armour-bearer refused; he dared not do it. Thereupon Saul took his own sword and fell on it. When the armour-bearer saw that Saul was dead, he too fell on his sword and died with him (REB).

The two suicides almost form a literary parallel with Abimelech. There is the dethroned and false king, the armor-bearer, the fear of dishonor, and of course the suicide.[10] Unlike Abimelech, however, Saul's armor-bearer refused the request, leaving the king to take matters into his own hands.[11] Once the act was accomplished, the armor-bearer did the same. One of the challenges for readers is determining Saul's reasoning, something that leads us into another connection with Abimelech. 1 Samuel 31:3 tells us King Saul was wounded (although "fear" may be the root word here), but unlike Abimelech, he had the ability to end his own life. As David Gunn has noted, Saul is refused even an honorable death in his last hours[12]—although, it is possible to read the actions of the Jabesh-Gileadites as an ironic twist of granting Saul, if not an honorable death, then at least an honorable burial.[13] It is Saul's case in rabbinic sources that gets special mention. In *Shulhan Arukh*, Y.D. 345.3, we read, "A leader who commits suicide under

10. Dragga, "In the Shadow," 43. Peter Leithart notes Saul died on Mount Gilboa, which he connects to religious cults. See Leithart, *Son to Me*, 155.

11. Edelman sees in the refusal an acknowledgement that Saul was still king (Edelman, *King Saul*, 286).

12. Gunn, *Fate of King Saul*, 111. Gunn notes that Saul's name was "in the best 'Roman' fashion."

13. Edelman, *King Saul*, 295.

compulsion, like King Saul, is not to be denied funeral honors." The *Genesis Rabbah* Midrash (34.13) sees Saul as the exception to the rule against suicide.[14]

A story in 2 Samuel 17 presents us with a suicide that could easily be mistaken for a Greco-Roman noble death.[15] Ahithophel, the wise advisor—first to King David and then to the usurper Absalom—gives advice to the rebel leader but seeing that it is denied, with great care ends his life. The apparent calculating action is without "explicit judgments concerning its moral rightness or wrongness."[16] As with before, there is a cosmological struggle. Ahithophel sees that his advice is ignored, not because he was wrong—rather, his counsel was understood to be divinely inspired, coming directly from God (2 Sam 16:23)—but because God refused to allow people to follow it (2 Sam 17:14).[17] The counselor now foresaw his end, leaving him no choice but to take an honorable path out. There is no commentary on the death within the text except that of the narrator's voice. Unlike the three before him, there is no motive assigned from the mouth of the victim.[18] It is, however, planned. If there is to be a lingering commentary, then it is that the deceased was granted an honorable burial.

After assassinating the drunken king Elah, Zimri took his place upon Israel's throne and promptly murdered what was left of the royal family. The soldiers of the southern kingdom cared little for this news and instead elected Omri, a commander of the force, their new king. After a short civil war (seven days, cf. 1 Kgs 16:15), Zimri, seeing that he would lose, retreated to the royal palace, and setting it on fire, burned alive as the ruins fell around him.[19] There is no great cosmic struggle here—rather, there is nothing reminiscent of theomachy—but there is the act of God's justice.

14. Cohen, *Sanctifying the Name of God*, 20–22

15. "La pendaison semble avoir été l'une des formes traditionnelles de suicide dans les classes inférieures de la société romaine" (Yolande, *Le suicide dans la Rome antique*, 108.

16. Bergen, *1, 2 Samuel*, 415–16.

17. Mays, *Harper's Bible Commentary*, 299.

18. The Sages of the Talmud suggest Ahithophel died to preserve his family's land. If he died a traitor after David's return to the throne, it is likely his property would have been forfeited (1 Kgs 21:15–16; cf. Sanhedrin 48b).

19. This account parallels the Babylonian account when the king of that empire, Shamash-shuma-ukin, lost to Ashurbanipal. See Matthews et al., *Old Testament*, 1 Kgs 16:18.

Zimri dies not simply for his sin but for the sins of the king he executed (1 Kgs 16:19).

The Maccabean books provided the early Christians with a great wealth of material for theological reflection of self-inflicted or self-chosen deaths. The first self-inflicted death in this series of books occurs when Eleazar rushes into a crowd of elephants to assassinate king Antiochus V:

> And Eleazaros Auaran saw one of the beasts plated with royal armor, and it stood above all the other beasts, and he thought that the king was on it. And he gave himself up (ἔδωκεν ἑαυτόν) to save his people and to secure for himself an everlasting name. (1 Macc 6:43–44, NETS)

In a less-than-ironic twist, the rather short episode accomplishes exactly what Eleazar meant to do, which is to preserve his name although we know that the sacrifice did nothing for his people.[20] The story of Eleazar did not cease to grow. Between 1 Maccabees (c. 150 BCE) and 3 Maccabees (c. late first century BCE) the story of the elephant slayer grew. In 3 Maccabees 6:16–19, Eleazar is pictured as piously recounting God's promises—specifically the promise to never abandon Israel—just before the attack (v. 18). Instead of the audience hearing only of the quick dash by the Jew, God and the heavenly host have now enjoined the battle (3 Macc 6:18). The story moves from a suicide for an unsuccessful but valiant reason (something like a noble death) to part of a rather dramatic cosmic battle of the gods.[21]

> Just as Eleazaros was bringing his prayer to an end, the king went by the hippodrome together with the beasts and all the pride of the force. At the sight of this, the Judeans cried out loudly to heaven so that even the nearby valleys resounded, causing frenzied terror throughout the entire army. Then the most glorious, Almighty and true God showed forth his holy face and opened the heavenly gates from which descended two glorious angels, terrible to behold, who were apparent to all except to the Judeans, and they withstood the force of the opponents and filled them with confusion and dread and bound them fast with shackles. (3 Macc 6:16–19, NETS)

Ptolemy Macron, Antiochus Eupator's general, is said to have "unable to execute his noble office honorably, he took poison and ended his life" (2 Macc 10:13, NETS). This may, on the surface appear to be a form of death,

---

20. He is mentioned in Gregory, *Mor.* 19.21.34, in regards to the morality of historical figures. Gregory sees his example as a positive one.

21. Eleazar's death can passively be seen in 3 Macc 6:23.

much like Ahithophel above. He had lost the respect of the leaders of his nation and, finding nothing else to live for, ended his own life. However, to include such a death in the Maccabean tradition should cause to examine him further. He was, after all, a Gentile. The disrespect stems from, not merely that he changed sides, but that he changed sides because he chose to treat the Jews with justice. If Macron is the same Ptolemy mentioned in 1 Maccabees 3:38 and 2 Maccabees 4:45, then the inclusion of 2 Maccabees 10:12 becomes more profound. Marcon begins his life as an enemy of the Jews, chosen by Lysais to eradicate Jewish opposition to the Greek king. Yet, he ends his life because of the mockery bestowed upon him for his turn at trying to treat the Jews with fairness before the law. To read it as a whole, Macron is a traitor not to Cyprus against Antiochus Eupator, but is a traitor to Antiochus against the Jews, and of course, the God of the Jews. The text affords little in regards to commentary on his death, only that he died because he chose to give the Jews justice. In a poetic (if not real) sense, he is a Gentile who died for the Jews.

Another suicide is found in 2 Maccabees, this time at 14:37–46, in which Razis, a loyal Jew who was soon to be arrested, killed himself because, "referring to die nobly (εὐγενῶς θέλων ἀποθανεῖν) rather than to fall into the hands of sinners and suffer outrages unworthy of his noble birth" (2 Macc 14:42, NETS). The phrase "εὐγενῶς θέλων ἀποθανεῖν"[22] is immediately noticeable expressly because of the praise it gives the suicidal Jew.[23] The details of the story must be examined almost minutely. Razis is a title, rather than a name, possibly derived from Isaiah 14:16–18 or 24.16 and related to his good standing in the community (2 Macc 14:17). As with Abimelech before him, a tower is involved (although it is doubtful the tower has a significance beyond the literary).[24] He is intent, as with King

22. Though only loosely related at best, see Aristotle, *Ethica Nicomachea* 1115b.5. A better connection—linguistically and contextually—can be found in Dionysius of Halicarnassus's work, *Roman Antiquities,* 10.46.5–6 (c. 30 BCE).

23. Both Jewish and Christian theologians have struggled with this passage. "The nobility was that of feeling, since nobility of birth was not recognized among the Jews. The justification and laudation of self murder, which here comes to light, is not only anti-Jewish, but has also been justly urged by Protestant theologians as directly militating against the canonicity of the present book. To this objection Roman Catholics have never been able to make a satisfactory answer. The cases of Saul and of Samson, sometimes cited as parallel, are in quite another category" (Lange et al., *Commentary on the Holy Scriptures,* 611).

24 Some scholars see the tower as part of the Temple. See Kampen, "Razis (Person)," 624.

Saul, refusing to allow any one or thing to stop him.[25] It is 14:46, however, that gives us more pause. After the horrific death, he dies with his entrails in hands proclaiming vindication in the Resurrection: "with his blood already completely drained from him, he tore out his entrails, took them in both hands and hurled them at the crowd, calling upon the Lord of life and spirit to give them back to him again. This was the manner of his death" (2 Macc 14:46, NETS).

Notably, there is the suicide of Judas (in Matthew's account, at least), which must be—because of the nature of the story in the Gospels and the close parallel to Jesus—examined more closely, even if only as a way to measure the literary reception of suicide.[26] Daube does not see in the story of Judas a crime but possibly as an atoning act.[27] Judas kills himself exactly because of remorse and, perhaps, in light of the Mosaic legal requirement found in Numbers 35:33 and Leviticus 24:17.[28] Augustine would disagree with that sentiment,[29] causing something of a disruption in his own theology of suicide and sin.[30] Jerome sees two crimes, with only one (suicide) necessary.[31] What was the remorse for? Several scholars have suggested

25. Bartlett, "2 Maccabees," 846–47.

26. It should be noted that the account in Acts 1:18 of Judas's self-inflicted death is reminiscent of Razis's final end. The tradition of Judas's death is contrary to Paul's view (1 Cor 15:5) and apocryphal sources (Gospel of Peter). For Papias, Judas did not die immediately but lingered on, eventually succumbing to death because of disease. Further, if we see Judas's death as a sacrificial death, we should see it in light of the Rabbinic prohibition against suicide exactly because they could not pay the debt of their soul (See Borchert, *John 1–11*, 299. Borchert cites Strack and Billerbeck, *Kommentar zum Neuen Testament* 1:1027–28). See below for a fuller discussion of Rabbinic allowances and prohibitions of suicide.

27. The fate of Judas has been preserved in Christian memory via several apocryphal gospels, one of which is the Coptic "Book of the resurrection of Jesus Christ," a work sometimes paired with the Gospel of Bartholomew. According to Hans-Josef Klauck, the harrowing story, of which Judas figures as one of the three remaining souls in Hades, predates the Gospel of Nicodemus, perhaps even to the second century. This is important given that it was not the suicide of Judas that prevented his escape, but his betrayal. See Klauck, *Apocryphal Gospels*, 99.

28. Daube, "Death as a Release," 88–89.

29. Augustine, *De civ. D.* 1.17.

30. See Pannenberg, *Anthropology in Theological Perspective*, 153. He writes, "But the reasons he gives—that suicide is a form of murder; that (as in the case of Judas) suicide expresses a despair of divine mercy; and that the suicide allows himself no chance to repent—do not connect suicide with the psychological analysis of sin as egoism and concupiscence."

31. Jerome, *Commentary on Matthew*, 4:27. Jerome sees suicide as necessary to fulfill

παραδίδωμι is directly related to the idea of a sacrifice.[32] If this is the case, that Judas is sacrificing Jesus, then we are meant to see the kiss as part of that sacrifice as well.[33] Perhaps this explains Judas's remorse, that he had sacrificed Jesus—meaning, that Judas's death is at least in some way connected to a cosmic struggle.

Notably absent in this chronological list is the story of Samson. The story of Samson, I maintain, does not fit easily into our already too-gray categories due to the existence in the story of a self-inflicted death and as well as the use of that death for external (revenge) reasons (i.e., sacrifice). Because of that, I will place Samson first in the category of self-inflicted death and examine him as such, but note that in the discussion of *devotio* he will be mentioned again.[34] Before Samson's life begins, it is announced via the angelical proclamation (Judg 13:2–20); however, there is nothing divine about him as a person. He does have great strength and a great mind, but this is due more to his vows than to a seminal merger of human and divine. After years of success against the Philistines, he succumbs to a trick by Delilah.

This is another event in Judges where a Jew dies in a contest between God and some foreign but cosmic adversary. In this case, the point is made

---

the biblical commandment against sinning against a fellow believer.

32. Berg, *Irony in the Matthean Passion*, 167–68; Koch, "Suicides and Suicide Ideation," 169. Παραδίδωμι was used by Herodotus to suggest a type of atoning sacrifice. "So spoke Cyrus, thinking that Darius was plotting against him; but in truth heaven was showing him that he himself was to die in the land where he was, and Darius to inherit his kingdom. So then Hystaspes answered him thus:—"Sire, the gods forbid that any Persian born should plot against you! but if such there be, may he speedily perish; for you have made the Persians freemen instead of slaves and rulers of all instead of subjects. But if your vision does indeed tell that my son is planning aught to your hurt, take him; he is yours to use as pleases you" (Herodotus, *Histories* 1.210). Closer to Judas's context, the 3rd aorist passive of παραδίδωμι is used in Greek Isaiah 53.12, διὰ τοῦτο αὐτὸς κληρονομήσει πολλούς, καὶ τῶν ἰσχυρῶν μεριεῖ σκῦλα· ἀνθ᾽ ὧν παρεδόθη εἰς θάνατον ἡ ψυχὴ αὐτοῦ, καὶ ἐν τοῖς ἀνόμοις ἐλογίσθη, καὶ αὐτὸς ἁμαρτίας πολλῶν ἀνήνεγκεν, καὶ διὰ τὰς ἀνομίας αὐτῶν παρεδόθη." See Houtman et al., *Actuality of Sacrifice*, 195, 195n7. If we take the kiss in light of Hosea 13:2, then we can see the connected between the kiss and the sacrifice.

33. Compare the kiss between Jesus and Judas to the one by Joseph to Jacob (Schwally, *Das Leben nach dem Tode*, 8) and 1 Kings 19:8 where Elijah attempts to find Israelites who had not "kissed" Baal.

34. I have to agree with Mays et al., that "Samson's death is not, strictly speaking, a suicide, since God grants his prayer for death, accepting him as an instrument through which to carry out the divine plan" (Mays et al., *Harper's Bible*, 258); however, with a broad definition of self-inflicted death is employed, then it does.

clear when the mocking of the God of the Israelites precedes the death of Samson (Judg 16:23–24; cf. 1 Kgs 18:40). If we compare this to the other suicides presented herein, it is the only one bearing the marks of a narrow definition of suicide. It is premeditated and planned.[35] He is led out and is placed between two pillars, feigning weakness—which should lead us against the notion of a noble death. After imploring God's help for vengeance against those who had blinded him, he begs his death be counted amount the Philistines.[36]

While the blindness may be symbolic here, it should be noted the revenge motive is rather personal. He dies not to save Israel or as an action devoted to God, but as a way to kill others for the wrong that had been enacted against him.[37] The whole of Samson's story is rather important because it not only summarizes the history of Israel's judges, but also the cyclical formation of the Book of Judges. Ironically, it is God's help allowing Samson to commit suicide, another part of the literary cycle since it is God's assistance that brings Samson into the world.

With the death of Samson, we see a continued theme of self-inflicted death intertwined with cosmic realities. The only possible non-cosmic suicides are the attendants to King Saul and Zimri. One could be considered cosmic, if King Saul was seen as a divine king but this is questionable given the portent against him. Zimri dies as a result of his sins and that of his forbearer. Eleazar does not begin his literary life as a cosmic suicide (1 Macc 6:43–44) but with a later rewrite is clearly part of the struggle in the skies between Rome and Jerusalem (3 Macc 6:16–19). Razis, depending upon the location ultimately assigned (tower, either in the Temple or his house) could be considered cosmic. As discussed above, the death of Judas is due to remorse, but remorse for what? If the kiss and the use of $\pi\alpha\rho\alpha\delta\acute{\iota}\delta\omega\mu\iota$ is related to a sacrifice, it could signal Judas's remorse for participating in a human sacrifice to either the God of the Jews or the Roman pantheon.

35. Note that Samson's death is not the only one planned. Ahithophel joins him in the list of those who with much forethought planned their death.

36. Because of this statement, Samson's death could be seen as a type of noble death. The Homeric Hecktor cries out just before his death, "Μὴ μὰν ἀσπουδί γε καὶ ἀκλειῶς ἀπολοίμην, Ἀλλὰ μέγα ῥέξας τι καὶ ἐσσομένοισι πυθέσθαι" (Homer, Illiad 23.304) while Arrians says of Alexander, "Μεγάλα ἔργα, καὶ τοῖς ἔπειτα πυθέσθαι ἄξια ἐργασάμενος οὐκ ἀσπουδεὶ ἀποθανεῖται" (De Exped. Alexand., 6.9).

37. It should be noted that chapter 16 begins with a different situation for Samson. In previous chapters, the Spirit of God was present yet here it is made clear that the Spirit of God had abandoned Samson, if not Israel as a whole. This connection of "the Spirit" and divine abandonment is something Paul uses in Galatians 3

Abimelech is pictured as fighting from the side of Baal against El. Samson wages war against Dagon. Ahithophel realizes God has declared war on him. Ptolemy Macron is the only Gentile in the list to die because of his service to the Jewish God on behalf of Israel.

There are several common denominators all share. The first is that they were successful in ending their own life by choice—and that such a death was met with no condemnation in the text. In some instances, the appreciation of their death grew in time. The second, and most importantly, is that each death is freely chosen even though a tension exists in the text whereby God ordains several of the deaths. God stirs up an evil spirit (of remembrance) against Abimelech. Saul's death is the result of his interaction with the witch of Endor (1 Sam 28:19). God had stopped Ahithophel's advice from being heard (2 Sam 17:14). The origin of Judas's death, however, is found in a prophecy from Jeremiah (Matt 27:9–10). While there is a tension between the free will and the control of God, it is neither remarked upon nor seemingly noticed.

Martyrdom

Self-inflicted death is not the only sort of chosen death mentioned in Scripture.[38] Likewise, there is the death chosen in lieu of violating God's law or as a witness to one's system of belief. It is too neat a dichotomy to suggest the suicides above occurred because of internal motives but the martyrdoms below are only external.[39] While the suicides are clearly a result of the choice of the individual based usually on some sense of honor, we cannot too easily separate the notion of blasphemy of a deity from that of personal honor.

38. Droge and Tabor, *Noble Death*, has rightly risen the ere of historians and historical ethicists, notably Darrel Amundsen, who argues against combining the categories of self-inflicted death and martyrdom. He writes "Droge and Tabor's determination to label such a diverse variety of motives and actions 'voluntary death' is so conspicuously special pleading and hence so entangles them in contradictions and inconsistencies that it becomes laughable" (Amundsen, "Significance of Inaccurate History," 10–11). While I may not go as far as Amundsen, I cannot side with Droge and Tabor. Rather, we have to allow that the shade of act and intent may appear to only barely separate the two, but in reality, provide for us a gulf of distinction.

39. The internal/external dichotomy is replaced below with "preservation" and "accomplishment." I argue that both martyrdom and suicide are often internal crises (as opposed to the *devotio*) meant to preserve something—honor (as in the case of suicide) or faithfulness to the covenant (i.e., Jewish identity).

Indeed, to dishonor one's parents, as in Leviticus 24:15–16, was conflated with blasphemy against God. While this development of the dual-honor system is not easily seen in the Mosaic Law, it becomes apparent with later writings, such as Ben Sira who writes, "He who glorifies father will prolong his days,and he who listens to the Lord will give rest to his mother" (Sir 3:6, NETS).[40] By the time we get to Rabbinical Judaism, the connection is fully developed so that Rabbis could say that God worked with parents to create the child, which is why to dishonor the parents is to blaspheme God. However, what may separate suicide from martyrdom for readers is the perception that suicide is for self-regarding reasons (internal) while martyrdom is for God or another good cause (external). Even then, we have those who cross the gray area such as the case of Ahithophel who may have died to preserve his estate for his progeny rather than his personal honor (such as a noble death). Regardless, even in martyrdom, a choice is often present even though it is not self-inflicted—thus allowing martyrdom something of a category of internal crisis, although as the martyr tradition develops, the dead take their place in the cosmic crisis (see Eleazar above).

The use of *martyr* to describe death because of religious persecution is not found in Jewish thought until the beginning of Christianity. However, there are stories of those who suffered and died because of their religious beliefs.[41] During the Second Temple period, suicide and martyrdom become somewhat mingled. For instance, the Jewish threat to Emperor Gaius includes not only the promise of a slaughter of the innocents but also suicide in protest of the proposed statue.[42] This has a recognizable history as part of the New Testament canon (specifically Heb 11). There is, of course, the religious death of the figure mentioned in Isaiah 52–53. Daniel records a possible massacre (Dan 11:29–34) with the promise of resurrection (Dan 12:1–3).[43] In the latter author's case, it is probable he is referring to the time of the Maccabees, at least *vaticinium ex eventu*. The same series of casualties

40. Blidstein, *Honor Thy Father and Mother*, 2–5.

41 F. F. Bruce suggests Abel is the first known martyr, a tradition in the Old Testament culminating with Zachariah. "In particular, it appears that Chronicles came at the end of the Bible which they used: when our Lord sums up all the martyrs of Old Testament times He does so by mentioning the first martyr in Genesis (Abel) and the last martyr in Chronicles (Zechariah). (See Luke 11:51 with 2 Chr 24:21)" (Bruce, "Canon of Scripture," 19–22).

42. Philo, *Legatio ad Gaium*, 236. See below.

43. The Book of Daniel contains two more stories of martyrdom, albeit unsuccessful martyrdoms (Dan 3; 6).

is recorded in the *Testament of Moses*. Perhaps the best-known execution tales escaping Second Temple Judaism is the story of the mother with seven sons (2 Macc 7; cf. 4 Macc 8; perhaps referenced in Heb 11:35–36) and Eleazar (2 Macc 6:18–31). Likewise, there is the death of John the Baptizer, Stephen, and even Paul—all considered martyred because they died by the hands of the state for their conviction to faithfulness. Josephus (*BJ* 7.320–406) records the suicidal martyrs at Masada, although in tones barely above that of his previous speech condemning those who take their own life.[44]

In this section, I will examine briefly the Maccabean martyr tradition. I will rely on Jarvis Williams's work, *Maccabean Martyr Traditions in Paul's Theology of Atonement,* in developing some of the allowances that martyrdom could be an atoning death—while maintaining the ultimate atonement made possible only by the *devotio* (contra to Williams) is not a type of martyrdom. Rather than delving into canonical examples of martyrdom, I believe it is better to focus on particularly those already identified as aiding the developing notion of an atoning death.

Another Eleazar is among those who chose to die, albeit this time as a choice made to avoid dishonor to God (as opposed to dishonoring himself).[45] The role of honor in Eleazar's choice to die is made explicit in 2 Maccabees 6:26–28 and the more so when he uses unambiguous language to describe the example he will leave beyond.[46] The author of 2 Maccabees is clear with phrases such as "But he, welcoming death with honor rather than life with pollution, went up to the rack of his own accord, spitting out the flesh, as all ought to do who have the courage to refuse things that it is not right to taste, even for the natural love of life" (2 Macc 6:19–20, NETS). But it is Eleazar's speech that is most telling.

> Even if for the present I would avoid the punishment of mortals, yet whether I live or die I shall not escape the hands of the Almighty. Therefore, by bravely giving up my life now, I will show myself worthy of my old age and leave to the young a noble example of how to die a good death willingly and nobly for the revered

---

44. It should be noted that the Rabbis refuse to speak of Masada. See Elon, "Politics and Archaeology," 45.

45. The previous Eleazar (as found in 1 Macc 6:43–44) seems to have been folded into the narrative here. We see this conflation in 3 Macc 6:1 when the Eleazar who is mauled by the elephants is misunderstood to be the Eleazar who is an aged priest. For the purpose of this study, I will not include 3 Maccabees as an account of the priestly Eleazar.

46. See Tilley, "Scripture," 383–97; van Henten, "Martyrdom and Persecution," 69–74, for the use of martyrdom stories as ways to create communities.

and holy laws." When he had said this, he went at once to the rack.
(2 Macc 6:26–28, NETS)

The story is retold in 4 Maccabees, but this time Eleazar is clearly pictured as a priest (4 Macc 5:4, 35).[47] Regardless, the accounts suggest the story of Eleazar has more to tell us than a mere reciting of an aged and pious claim. In 2 Maccabees, he is said to have a "προσώπου κάλλιστος."[48] As we will see in chapter 4, this aura of the victim is important to recognize. Further, there is the cosmic scope of the example.[49] Eleazar, while not giving us a reason to believe in the resurrection (cf. Heb 11:35), does understand that his death will have a greater ramification. He acknowledges that he will never escape God, but sees that his ultimate end will be a model—but there is no mention of an atoning aspect or any cosmic aspect to his death. He chooses to make it an instance to piety, thus aiding, or rather, cooperating in God's ultimate victory only as a true witness.

Of particular note is 2 Maccabees 6.1. We are introduced to an exact concept that may play a part in Paul's use of the *devotio* in Galatians. The phrase, "πατρῷοι νόμοι," would have been noticeable to the non-Jewish Greek reader and would have caused immediate displeasure. It was simply against cultural standards to force anyone to violate their "πατρῷοι νόμοι."[50] The phrase is repeated several times throughout 2 Maccabees 6–7, becoming an almost-creedal statement of their cause of their death.[51] They refused to violate that most sacred principle. It is possible we see something of this in Paul's description of himself as found in Galatians 1:14 ("τῶν πατρικῶν

47. It is possible "γραμματεύς" (2 Macc 6:18) means only a low level attendant, perhaps merely a Levite rather than a priest. However, given the visage assigned to Eleazar, it is little doubt that he was meant to be seen, at the very least, as a leading holy attendant of the Temple. See Schürer, *History*, 2:322–25; Himmelfarb, *Kingdom of Priests*, 11–52; Stern, *Studies*, 97n119; Schwartz, *Studies*, 89–101.

48. See 2 Macc 6:23 as well. The advanced age and the ἐπιφανής of his appearance are noted several times in several ways.

49. If cosmology seems to be a muted concept in the first conception of Eleazar, it becomes predominant in 2 Macc 7.

50. See Schwartz, *2 Maccabees*, 285, who recommends seeing Renaud, "Loi et lois"; Kippenberg, *Erlösungsreligionen*, 206–9; Schröder, *Die 'väterlichen Gesetze,'* 207–12, on 2 Maccabees.

51. Goldstein seems to see this as a clash of monotheists against polytheists, which is not necessarily true (Goldstein, *2 Maccabees*, 282). Rather, it is not about the notion of one deity above or against the many, but about the covenant with a deity and the attempted coercion to violate it. I do not see in these stories the attempt to make this an issue of the number of deities.

μου παραδόσεων"). If this were the case, that "πατριοι νόμοι" plays a part in Galatians, then it should be assumed that to employ a martyrdom theology in Galatians, Paul would need Jesus to have died for the ancestral law rather than, as he says, to bring it to an end. Given the prevalence of "πατριοι νόμοι" in the Maccabean martyr tradition but finding it absent in Galatians, it is doubtful Paul saw Jesus as another in the line of martyrs.

Another peculiarity surrounding the martyrdom tradition is the issue of divine abandonment, even if the nature of a very present but absent deity is on the surface, contradictory. In 5:17, divine abandonment is the explicit reason Antiochus had an almost free reign to persecute the Jews. We read, "Antiochus was elated in spirit and did not perceive that the Lord was angered for a little while because of the sins of those who lived in the city and that this was the reason he was disregarding the place" (NETS). However, Eleazar urges the opposite view in 6:16, saying, "Therefore he never withdraws his mercy from us. While he disciplines us with calamities, he does not forsake his own people" (NETS).[52]

The second martyrdom in 2 Maccabees is the account of the seven brothers who died in successive, grueling, order under torturous circumstances.[53] The mother simply dies.[54] They too refused to eat pork or break the Law of Moses.[55] Each death brought a small speech, but the final brother

---

52. Schwartz notes, "the author subtly revises his message in this regard, moving, in his explanation of how the Jews can suffer, from God turning His face away in anger to God chastising His people as a father chastises His sons" (Schwartz, 2 *Maccabees*, 284). Even this presents too neat a line between divine abandonment and divine punishment, as discussed in chapter 2.

53. Note the contrast between the elderly Eleazar and the youthful brothers.

54. In 4 Maccabees, the mother, to avoid being touched by the guards, threw herself into the fire (4 Macc 17:1).

55. Goldstein notes the odd use of the devices of torture, specifically measures meant to extract information or to punish for treason. He writes, "Torture in antiquity was employed usually for two purposes: to get information and to punish serious offenses such as treason. . . . If the purpose was only to get information, the authorities might avoid inflicting irreparable damage on the victim. Accordingly, when the victims here find themselves only whipped, they assume that the king intends to question them (vs. 2). In fact, the king's intention in whipping them was probably not at all to elicit information, but to coerce them to obey." The entirety of the scene, then, becomes more gruesome when one considers the choices made by both king and martyr requiring the deaths. While there is a sense of freedom of choice here, and it is real, it is also likewise a mistake to assume there were any other choice but death. Goldstein concludes, "Thus it is strange that the second brother (and he alone), after being irreparably mutilated, is given the opportunity to change his mind (vs. 7)" (Goldstein, 2 *Maccabees*, 304).

is the one who almost neatly summarizes the whole.[56] In 2 Maccabees, it is reported that he says,

> For we are suffering because of our own sins. And if our living Lord is angry for a little while, to rebuke and discipline us, he will again be reconciled with his own slaves. But you, unholy wretch, you most defiled of all mortals, do not be elated in vain and puffed up by uncertain hopes, when you raise your hand against the children of heaven. You have not yet escaped the judgment of the Almighty, all-seeing God. For our brothers, after enduring a brief suffering, have fallen heir to everlasting life under the power of a divine covenant, but you, by the judgment of God, will receive just punishment for your arrogance. I, like my brothers, give up body and life for our ancestral laws, appealing to God to show mercy soon to our nation and by torments and plagues to make you acknowledge that he alone is God and through me and my brothers to bring to an end the wrath of the Almighty that has justly fallen on our whole nation. (2 Macc 7:30–38, NETS).

It is the final few lines driving martyr theology as it is clear the author wishes the audience to remember the deaths of the brothers (as compared to that of Eleazar) as a sacrifice to avert God's wrath.[57] They avert the wrath begun by the Hellenization by instead refusing to subvert the Law of Moses: "ἕτοιμοι γὰρ ἀποθνῄσκειν ἐσμὲν ἢ πατρῴους νόμους παραβαίνειν" (2 Macc 7:2).[58] What is missing is the overt insistence upon the resurrection

---

56. There seems to be a connection between each brother's speech and the next, as if the one diatribe against the Gentile king is given seven parts. See Mays et al., *Harper's Bible Commentary*, 907.

57. Both stories in 2 Maccabees, taken together, are designed to present a counter to the rebellion found in 1 Maccabees. Whereas in 1 Maccabees 160–64 and 2:32–38 it is Judas's valor saving the Jews, now we have the call to merely withstand. It is this withstanding (two choices in one, with the first not to fight and the second not to bend) that causes blood to be spilled which in turn averts the wrath of God. There can be little doubt about the connection between these two segments in 2 Maccabees and the brief summaries in 1 Maccabees, however, the role the deaths take remains untethered. Goldstein argues that a common source underlies 1 and 2 Maccabees. As with other common source theories, the argument is based on something not present, namely the supposed common source. See Goldstein, *2 Maccabees*, 269–70, 284. For other discussions on the use of 2 Maccabees as counter to 1 Maccabees, see Nickelsburg, *Resurrection*, 98, and Stern, "Relations between Judaea and Rome" 21n119.

58. J. Williams sees these sacrifices as "atoning sacrifices and as a saving event for Israel," following the example he believes is in Isaiah 53 whereby a martyr "died for Israel to atone for their sin and to save the nation from God's wrath" (Williams, *Maccabean Martyr Traditions*, 43). There is little doubt that the deaths are presented in such a way as

(although, see v. 36), but this is found in verse 9 where one brother sees it as the reward for the present sufferings.[59] Indeed, the seven brothers, unlike Eleazar, provide a sacrifice for καταλλάσσω (2 Macc 7:33), signifying the end of the divine abandonment, or punishment. This is understood given the turnaround in 8:1–3. As with Eleazar above (and with Paul's letter), the underlying premise here is a connection to Deuteronomy.[60]

Of note is the use of ἀπολύω. In 7:9, the second brother declares that death is the real freedom—the freedom to be rewarded with everlasting life. This is, as Schwartz points out, the reverse of Eleazar's compatriot's suggestion in 6:22.[61] In the former, ἀπολύω is something purchased with deceit and available to the living. In the latter, it is the reward after death for obeying God. Indeed, ἀπολύω is immediately connected to the concept of ἀναβίωσις. In the final speech, it is clearer that the death of the martyr is covenantal in scope, "ἐπενέγκαντες πόνον ζωῆς ὑπὸ διαθήκην θεοῦ πεπτώκασιν."[62] It is without a doubt that the concepts of freedom and covenant are intertwined, whether or not life and death are the starting points for the discussion.

Even a cursory reading of the Maccabean martyr texts causes one to consider a deep connection to Paul's images of atonement—much more than any image of suicide. If one was to step back and examine the martyrs by broad-stroke, the stories have many of the points of the *devotio*—except the divine victim (Eleazar comes the closest) *and* the stories exceed the requirements by requiring the victim to die to prevent an attack on God's

to act as deterrent. However, Williams is adamant of two things. One, that the deaths are not like the Greco-Roman counterparts (something he examines on 33–37), in dying to appease a plethora of gods and two, that this non-Greco-Roman viewpoint is the basis of Paul's understanding of the death of Jesus. Given the nature of 2 Maccabees itself, the fact that particular language is used to appeal to Greco-Roman audiences, and that the line between appeasement and diverse is too narrow to fully notice, his case is circumstantial at best.

59. Also present, but not important to our particular study, is the role the "Hebrew language" plays in the response to the king, to be compared to Jesus on the cross (cf. Mark 15:33).

60. Schwartz, *2 Maccabees*, 299. Deuteronomy 31 and 32 play a large role in these two chapters of 2 Maccabees.

61. Schwartz, *2 Maccabees*, 304. While this has a Platonic sense, as Schwartz rightly notes, I do not believe it is the weighted goal.

62. Schwartz translates this as "have come into God's covenant of eternal life" citing several scholars who disagree regarding the genitive. Regardless of the final construction of the phrase, the suffering is connected to the covenant (which is connected to abandonment or punishment) and thus to eternal life.

honor. However, with just a small amount of manipulation, martyr theology could easily include *devotio* in some way.[63] While Williams has identified a martyr theology in the various stories (including their expansions in 4 Maccabees), he offers a rather broad definition that, while bearing striking resemblance to Greco-Roman counterparts, ignores the proximity and by doing so, misses several points that would aid his interpretation. In missing the vindication of the martyrs, he leaves room to apply his theology to Paul's atoning image.[64]

Leon Morris, before Williams, argued against the use of martyr theology to view the image of Jesus.[65] Stanley Porter follows suit.[66] Brian McLean rejects martyrdom wholesale based on Galatians 3:13.[67] While bearing striking similarities to *devotio*, the use of Maccabean martyrdom in understanding the voluntary death of Jesus is not what Paul has in mind (at least) in Galatians. A deep understanding of the way linguistic nuance works is paramount in understanding the difference between martyrdom and *devotio* and how it is the latter that better frames the death of Jesus. However, what the martyrdom traditions do allow is the allowance of a voluntary death if given the right circumstances such as honoring God's commands.[68] Further, as we have seen, there is the cosmic crisis connotation, something we will see as we explore Christian martyr traditions and the *devotio*.[69]

63. As discussed in chapter 4, *devotio* is a sacrifice not for a cause, people, or other institution as much as it is for a victory. The *devotio* is as much about the victim as it is for the victory.

64. Specifically in Galatians, we cannot find a concern with the vindication of the death of Jesus as we do in 2 Maccabees 6–7. In other words, there is no narrative in Galatians suggesting Jesus threatened to be raised on God's day of judgment if he was killed.

65. Morris, "Meaning," 3–43. See Morris, *Apostolic Preaching*, 32–33, 194–95.

66. Porter, "Reconciliation," iii–iv, 175–78, 188–89.

67. McLean, "Absence of Atoning Sacrifice," 531–53. McLean sees the death of Christ as a *pharmakos*, something not completely uncommon (see chapter 1); however, as the death of Christ in Galatians is meant to bring reconciliation, McLean's use of the image stops start of the military imagery needed to round out the interpretation. For the military imagery surrounding reconciliation, see Breytenbach, "Salvation of the Reconciled," 271–86.

68. Williams gives a succinct history of the development of the discussion around the Maccabean martyr theology and the image of atonement in Williams, *Maccabean Martyr Traditions*, 6–26.

69. To note, "cosmic crisis" does not necessitate a civil war (as we see between God and Israel and later, between the Roman deities). Rather, cosmic crisis, particular in the situation of the martyrs is likely a type of divine wrath, or better, divine absence in which God is purposely allowing Israel to experience exile as a form of punishment.

Devotio is separated from martyrdom in the fact that martyrdom is an event or situation forced upon the victim—even if they choose to ultimately die—with no overarching or long reaching outcome intended. For example, the martyrs mentioned above chose to die only as a way to maintain their Jewish identity—with the crisis often internal or at the very least, personal.[70] The victim here dies to preserve something (much as we have seen in suicide; see above). Not every dire situation will produce a martyr, and no martyr is born to expressly be a martyr. However, it is the victim in *devotio* that is born divine (or made divine) in order to have the free will required to choose a voluntary and sacrificial death in order to bring an end to an external cosmic crisis. The victim's identity in this instance is completed only in the act of sacrifice and the victim dies in order to accomplish something.

Human Sacrifice

Under the rather broad term of sacrifice, I want to limit it to human sacrifice—this is, the giving of a person's life resulting in death, either by an external party or through a personal choice, with the intent to *appease* a deity or to force them to act on behalf of the victim.[71] Human sacrifice is usually thought to be roundly condemned in the Jewish Scriptures, with this prohibition seemingly reaching back to antiquity as it is found in the various strains of the Torah. For instance, it is found in the Levitical codes (Lev 20:1–3) as well as the Deuteronomistic school (Deut 12:31; 18:10; 2 Kgs 21:6). It is a sign of outside deities and foreign corruption (2 Kgs 23:20–25; Jer 7:31; Ezek 20:25–26). Strikingly, however, it is also part of the appeasement to the Israelite deity (Exod 22:29). In this section, I will present a list of human sacrifices, drawn from Paul's possible Jewish literary sources, in order to show that its positive efficacy would not be foreign to Paul, his Jewish readers, or readers of the Jewish texts. This list is not meant to be comprehensive, only intended to showcase events I deem necessary to understanding the allowance for human sacrifice by Paul's God.

70. Or in another way, the martyr chooses to allow someone to kill them while the *devotio* victim chooses to force someone to kill them, thus choosing to force someone into cooperating with them to offer up the victim as a sacrifice.

71. In this way, human sacrifice is not much different than martyrdom except in what it accomplishes (the intent). See Williams, *Maccabean Martyr Traditions*, 84. If it is self-sacrifice, then we have to ask how it is different than suicide. On the whole, we can only argue intent when deciding how a self-inflicted death is to be categorized.

I begin with Exodus wherein we find at least two accounts of human sacrifice. In Exodus 22 we have deaths required for witchcraft, bestiality, and sacrifices to other gods (Exod 22:18–20) along with the requirement to surrender the first born of both human and animal. These crimes are related in that they represent the movement of the Israelite away from the covenant of and allegiance to YHWH. In such, they should be taken as a whole, with each successive penalty understood as an expansion. As such, the rendering of Hebrew Exodus 22:20 is extremely important and can be seen as a form of devotion, or sacrifice to appease the deity.[72] That such a devotion was required shortly before the surrendering of the first-born cannot be seen as a mere redaction-related coincidence. The sacrifice in Exodus 22:29–30 is often seen as a fertility rite, as in other ANE cultures the first-born (at least of livestock) would be sacrificed to insure future gains.[73] This first-born devotion is seen in Leviticus 27:28–29, particularly in the last phrase. These devotions were human sacrifice, sometimes including the entire household, meant to appease the deity.[74]

We find several examples of human sacrifice in Numbers. The first is a vow made to Israel's deity to devote an entire people if the land was given to them. This action, as Wenham notes, follows Deuteronomy 7 and 9 as well as Joshua (6:21, for instance) in annihilating the inhabitants to prevent apostasy.[75] Likewise, this proscription follows Leviticus 27:28–29.[76] The second is an appeasement to the deity while the other could better qualify as a *devotio* offered as a reward (see below). In Numbers 25 we read of the men

---

72. The Hebrew reads ":וְגֵר לֹא־תוֹנֶה וְלֹא תִלְחָצֶנּוּ כִּי־גֵרִים הֱיִיתֶם בְּאֶרֶץ מִצְרָיִם" while the Greek reads, "Ὁ θυσιάζων θεοῖς θανάτῳ ὀλεθρευθήσεται, πλὴν Κυρίῳ μόνῳ." Dozeman translates the Hebrew as: "Anyone who sacrifices to gods, other than Yahweh alone, will be devoted to destruction" (Dozeman, *Exodus*, 522). The Greek is less pointed, although some of the word order is preserved.

73. Matthews et al., *Old Testament*, Exod 22:29.

74. "In some cases their families and their property were also destroyed in a general purging of evil. They have committed acts that violate God's holiness and contaminate the community. Therefore their sentence must be carried out without exception. Only in this way can God's name be restored to its proper sanctity and the people be cleansed of their impurity" (Matthews et al., *Old Testament*, Lev 27:29–33)

75. Wenham, *Numbers*, 174–75.

76. Milgrom writes, "'Proscription' is succinctly and accurately defined by P. D. Stern as 'consecration through destruction.' This definition defies its usual understanding as a form of taboo. The proscription attested in the Bible is exercised by Israel against other nations as the result of either a vow (Num 21:2–3) or God's command (Num 25:16–18; 31:1–12), or against its own rebels" (See Milgrom, *Leviticus*, 330–31).

of Israel having sexual intercourse with Moabite women and participating in Moabite worship (Baal of Peor).[77] This is in direct violation of the laws specifically mentioned above and is thus seen as an apostasy[78]—something the deity answered by ordering the men to be killed before him to avert the anger (the wrath that would kill twenty-four thousand).[79] The tenor of the original language indicates a very real possibility that there is a cultic ritual in mind behind the entire display.[80] This scene also establishes the son of Eleazar as a priest, leading us into the situation found in Numbers 31, whereby a victorious Israel was commanded to surrender a portion of the now-conquered Midianites. Only 32 men were given to the priests for the deity, leaving us to wonder if this surrendering was to die or to work.[81]

At first glance our next passage may not be directly connected to Numbers 25 and 31, however, Ezekiel's retelling of Israelite history horridly interrupts at the point of the wilderness apostasy to proclaim that God would cause them to sacrifice their children. I am not convinced this is the case. The interpretations of Ezekiel 20:25–26 are plentiful, many with merit.[82] Hahn and Bergsma, like others, point to העביר as the phrase that begins the interpretation stratification.[83] They refute the possible interpretation that sees this as pointing to child sacrifice by, in part, listing the other places the Hebrew word is found in Ezekiel—at no point is the word used

77. It is possible the zibḥê ʾĕlōhêhen of the second verse points to an Israelite participation in human sacrifice, which refocuses the entire scene. See the general discussion in Heider, Cult of Molek, 388–89.

78. According to Gray, "The women not unnaturally summon their paramours to their feasts, which, according to ancient custom, were sacrificial occasions; in partaking of the feast the Israelites honoured the god" (Gray, Numbers, 381–82).

79. Phinehas was given a pledge by God for his loyalty, so that his family line would be priests forever. As Knierim notes, this pledge calls to mind the ordination of the Levitical priesthood. As with other forms of sacrifice, it is possible to see this as an offering to God without an agreed upon term, only that God does in fact give the priest something as a reward. See Knierim, Numbers, 4:265.

80. In Milgrom, Numbers, the author see a possibility for sacrifice at the sanctuary but would argue against, while allowing that what is clearly seen here involves a ritual of some sort, a ritual for "expiation for Israel's apostasy." See Milgrom, "Shok Haterumah," 1–11; "Tenufah," 38–55; Studies in Cultic Theology, 140, 160–61 (cited in Milgrom, Numbers, 213.

81. Milgrom, Numbers, 263.

82. See Block, Ezekiel, 639–41. One of the key disagreements revolves around the state of the text. Several scholars seek to show that the present text is faulty, although Greek Ezekiel does share the same meaning.

83. Hahn, "What Laws Were 'Not Good'?," 211.

in conjunction with children; however, in this instance, it is.[84] While Hahn and Bergsma look to the retelling of the Exodus account, it may be better to place the stark interruption in Numbers, given the possibility of an Israelite apostasy of, at least, child sacrifice as well as the sacrifice during the plague. If Ezekiel is retelling the Torah narrative, then we are not limited to reading only Exodus as the literary backdrop. If this is read next to Numbers 25, the passage becomes gruesomely clear—and well within Ezekiel's descriptions of how God acts in judging his people.

1 Kings 13:2 finds completion in 2 Kings 23:20. As with other passages, there is some concern, seemingly, to preserve the ideal that the Israelite cult excluded human sacrifice. For instance, Walton, et al., is quick to see the bones as that of the already deceased.[85] However, 2 Kings 23:20 includes a reference to the sacrifice upon the altar of priests not dedicated to the Israelite deity.[86] This is maintained both in the Hebrew[87] and the Greek.[88] Further, it is supported as an act in succession—beginning with scattering human bones, burning then, and then offering up the bones with living flesh still on them.[89] Further, it is possible that this act was done to mirror the actions of the Moloch worships (cf. Jer 7:30–34; 19:10–13).[90]

There are two final examples I will offer as examples. The first is found in Deuteronomy 13:13–18. The description of the land *after* exile is meant to connect to the events when Israel first invaded Canaan, in which *devotio* occurred. As Goldingay notes,

> Yhwh's giving land to Israel involves taking it from other peoples
> . . . the dominant First Testament account portrays Yhwh taking a
> land from its occupants. The story makes the point very strongly
> by the verbs it uses to describe the process. It involves effacing

84. See Klein, 2 *Chronicles*, 396–97; Heider, "Molech (Deity)," 897; Davis, "Self-Consciousness and Conversation," 31; Stager and Wolff, "Child Sacrifice at Carthage," 31–51, as a small representation of scholars who see the possibility of child sacrifice in Ezekiel 20:25–26.

85. Matthews et al., *Old Testament*, 1 Kgs 13:2.

86. I note Matthews et al. do not comment on 2 Kgs 23:20.

87. וַיִּזְבַּח אֶת־כָּל־כֹּהֲנֵי הַבָּמוֹת אֲשֶׁר־שָׁם עַל־הַמִּזְבְּחוֹת וַיִּשְׂרֹף אֶת־עַצְמוֹת אָדָם עֲלֵיהֶם וַיָּשָׁב יְרוּשָׁלָם

88. καὶ ἐθυσίασεν πάντας τοὺς ἱερεῖς τῶν ὑψηλῶν τοὺς ὄντας ἐκεῖ ἐπὶ τῶν θυσιαστηρίων καὶ κατέκαυσεν τὰ ὀστᾶ τῶν ἀνθρώπων ἐπ' αὐτά, καὶ ἐπεστράφη εἰς Ιερουσαλημ.

89. Dearman, "Tophet in Jerusalem," 65–66.

90. See Dearman, "Tophet in Jerusalem," 66.

(kā☒ad hiphil), tearing down (hāras piel), expelling (gāraš qal and piel) and confounding *(hāmam)* (e.g., Exod 23:23–31). It involves clearing out *(nāšal)*, striking down (nākâ hiphil), breaking down (nāta☒), shattering (šābar piel), cutting up (gāda☒ piel), burning (śārap), dispossessing (yāraš qal and hiphil), devoting by killing (☒āram hiphil), finishing (kālâ piel), destroying (šāmad hiphil), eliminating (☒ābad piel and hiphil) and cutting off (kārat hiphil) (e.g., Deut 7:1, 2, 5, 17, 20, 22, 24; 12:2, 3, 29).[91]

Reading Deuteronomy 13:13–18 in this light, we see a proscription (see above) that, while not carried out in post-exilic times, nevertheless would have given the reader ample opportunity to discover vows and humans devoted in a cultic manner to God. There is a view here that this is merely corporate punishment—and that should not be discarded—however, if we compare this scene with that of Achan (Josh 7:20–21), it is about a penal sacrifice more so than retributive punishment.[92]

The final example is, perhaps, the most well known—the tale of the daughter of Jephthah (Judg 11:30–31). Further, this pericope is likewise tangentially connected in character and action with Numbers 21 (see above).[93] We have to first begin by understanding vows according to the Torah (Gen 28:20–22; Lev 27:2–13; Num 30:2–15)—made to a deity and with serious expectation of fulfillment.[94] The Hebrew נֶדֶר (usually translated in the Greek as εὐχή) is one that is always made as an act towards God in the Hebrew bible, usually for something in return[95] and is different than an oath.[96] Of particular note, the use of this word in surrounding cultures usually pointed to human sacrifice,[97] which is why we cannot allow that the

---

91. Goldingay, *Old Testament Theology*, 475. See his comments on Numbers 21:21–35 (Goldingay, *Old Testament Theology*, 478).

92. For punishment rather than sacrifice, see Thompson, *Deuteronomy*, 195. See also Tigay, *Deuteronomy*, 135.

93. It is not happenstance the Ammonites are characters in or near stories where votive offerings of humans are made to the Israelite deity. For a brief report of the connection, see Boling, "Jephthah (Person)," 681–82.

94. For an interpretation of expected fulfillment, see Schiffman, "Law of Vows and Oaths," 199–214.

95. Lowery, "Oaths and Vows."

96. Collins and Attridge, *Mark*, 310–11.

97. Jenni and Westermann, *Theological Lexicon*, 719. For a connection to *ban* as well as the expectation of sacrifice in light of the Moabite neighbors, see Collins, "Zeal of Phinehas," 5–6.

Israelite Judge expected anything other than a *human* to walk out his door.[98] In regards to vows, we must conclude that the Hebrew text allows that Jews could bargain with their deity, but only by offering some sort of sacrifice—a sacrifice that could have been human.[99]

Where there are more devotions of humans in the Jewish texts Paul was likely to use,[100] the ones selected above represent what is most important in deciphering Paul's theological allowances—that the Hebrew bible was not unfamiliar with Jewish human sacrifice in the service of God. Further, we have also seen that the concept of votive offerings, that of laying a requirement that entraps the deity to action on the side of the Jews. In this next section, we will explore Jewish reaction to this issue as a way of understanding the Jewish interpretation matrix in which Paul lived and wrote.

Thus far, we have seen the Jewish books give clear demonstrations of self-inflicted deaths as well as martyrdoms and human sacrifice. The books themselves contain little to no exploration or offer reflection of these events, unless we count the expansion of the stories as found in the Maccabean tetralogy. What is rather clear is the written works readily accepted that sometimes, it was just as necessary to take one's own life in the service of God just as it was to take another's.

Excursus

The examples below are, at best, non-canonical. They are not so easily seen as suicide but should be counted as the possibility, given the reasons specified below. The primary text of the Septuagint supports a close translation from the Hebrew available to us in the MT.[101] The "B" recension presents a different couplet somewhat transforming the meaning of several passages

98. Moore, *Judges*, 299. See also, Matthews et al., *Old Testament*, Judg 11:31.

99. As one scholar notes, this scene—this bargaining—may reflect that Jephthah did not have confidence in God, and likewise that God did not care for Jephthah as a judge. If we move this further along this line of thinking, then the judge, lacking confidence in God, make a vow that trapped the deity. The deity, not wanting to be trapped, insured that the daughter (rather than the expected throngs of jubilant Jews) would greet her father. See Biddle, *Reading Judges*, 127.

100. For instance, there are two kings of Israel who would later do the same (2 Kgs 16:3; 21:6) in what would later become known as Gehenna. I chose not to use these given that unlike the rest, they are condemned in the text.

101. I am using Rahlf's text. He has based "B" on Codex Vaticanus.

in Judges 5, notably 5:2.[102] It reads, "Ἀπεκαλύφθη ἀποκάλυμμα ἐν Ἰσραήλ· ἐν τῷ ἀκουσιασθῆναι λαὸν εὐλογεῖτε Κύριον." The phrase "τῷ ἀκουσιασθῆναι" is often translated as "volunteer"; however, if we compare the use of this word to other translation strategies employed in the Septuagint, then we cannot understand the word as merely a description of a draft-less army, but must wonder if it does not point to offering one's self, even if that offering is a sin.

As we will see, Jewish thought developing from the Second Temple period onward forbade offering oneself for death. Yet, we have a passage suggesting that because several tribes did, there was a revelation in Israel. Further, the song is replete with imagery of the sacrifice in the name of a god or gods (5:8), a problem for any rabbinic Jew. If the translator is honest with both the text and the developing tradition against cultic sacrifice for any reason, then how might he have worded his translation? If 5:2 is translated as an interpretative strategy to either smooth the roughness of a Hebrew *Vorlage* or to make a theological statement, then perhaps the translator borrowed a previous translator's choice to do so.

We should read Judges 5:2 next to Numbers 15:24–28, which reads,

> And it shall be, if it happens unintentionally outside the eyes of the congregation, all the congregation shall also do one unblemished calf from the cattle as a whole burnt offering, as an odor of fragrance to the Lord, and the sacrifice of this and its libation according to instruction and one male goat from the goats for sin. And the priest shall make atonement for all the congregation of Israel's sons, and it shall be forgiven them because it is unintentional. And they themselves have brought their gift as an offering to the Lord for their sin before the Lord, for their unintentional sins. And it shall be forgiven with respect to all the congregation of Israel's sons and for the guest who attaches himself to you, because for all the people it is unintentional. Now if one soul sins unintentionally, he shall bring forward one year–old female goat for sin. the priest shall make atonement concerning the soul that acts unintentionally and sins unintentionally before the Lord, to make atonement for him. (Num 15:24–28, NETS)

The ἀκουσιάζομαι matches the Hebrew שגג in Numbers 15:28. Indeed, several related Greek words are aligned neatly with the Hebrew. If we

---

102. As Philip E. Satterthwaite points out, Judges 5 (LXX) offers several examples of creative retranslations to smooth over the nonsensical Hebrew *Vorlage*. (See his introduction to Judges in NETS 197).

read Judges with the passage in Numbers, we can offer a better supposition to the translator's choice for his Greek. The march to war, which required soldiers to volunteer themselves to die in the name of a god, was a sin (albeit one of ignorance, or perhaps, against the will but necessary) because it involved the sacrifice of the person to the deity. However, because it was required, it was forgiven (via an atonement ritual) and celebrated. Because of the self-sacrifice of the soldiers, God awarded Israel victory.

While there is no evidence of Paul's use of Judges in Galatians, there is plenty of suggestive indications Paul had access to Judges and shared some of the theology found therein.[103] Given the connection between this recension of Judges 5:2 and Numbers 15:24–28, it is possible there exists wider application of atonement and the sin of ignorance in Second Temple Judaism.

In 1 Maccabees 9:54–56, we see a story of the pro-Hellenist priest, Alcimus. In a later document, the *Genesis Rabbah*, we see the story of Jaqim of Serorot.[104] In the Maccabean recounting of the story, the Priest has a stroke after attempting to destroy the wall separating Jew and Gentile. However, in *Genesis Rabbah* 42 and *Midrash Tehillim*, the death becomes a suicide by hanging on a pole. That this is in *Genesis Rabbah* is noteworthy given the interpretation of Isaac's death in 56:3. Given the statement in Ephesians 2:14, it is possible later Jewish exegetes saw in this story an Anti-Christian typology.[105]

RABBINIC REACTION

In regards to the various forms of voluntary death, the Rabbis are often disjointed interpreters, showing some semblance to others who sought to rationalize what appeared to be a heinous self-victimizing crime. If we take voluntary death broadly but under the roughly established concept of suicide, we can then follow Jonathan Goldstein's allowance of differing views

103. For some discussion on Paul's use of not simply citation, but theology from a wider ranger of the Jewish scriptures, see Ciampa, *Presence and Function*.

104 I am indebted for this translation to Baumgarten, *Studies in Qumran Law*, 174–75.

105. The role of *Genesis Rabbah* as polemic has already been noted by Jacob Neusner (Neusner, "Genesis Rabbah as Polemic," 253–65. Along these lines is Neusner's other suggestion that the commentary provided by this ancient work on Genesis 9:5 somewhat changes Jewish views on suicide.

held by Jewish commentators.[106] Because of the necessity of limiting the scope more to voluntary death rather than categorizing it as I have above—and because, as we will, the Jews likely only had two categories, I will focus in this section on establishing the existence and allowance thereof by post-Second Temple Jewish interpreters.

It appears Rabbinic Judaism quickly forbade suicide, as exemplified by Rabbi Eleazar's interpretation of Genesis 9:5 forbidding the taking of one's life.[107] Voluntary death—even in some instances, martyrdom—became the same as murder and as such, later rabbis compassionately turned to deal with the intentionality and culpability.[108] Indeed, if the motivation was repentance, then the crime is atoned for by the intention.[109] The intention could even be to avoid suffering, such as in the case of Rabbi Hanina ben Teradiyon. In this case, Teradiyon refused to breathe in the smoke caused by the flames of the pyre upon which he was tied, fearing that by doing so, he would be considered a suicide.[110] Rabbi Hananyah, an onlooker, took it upon himself to bribe the executioners to speed the process along. This example, rather than serving to prevent voluntary death (supporting Teradiyon's decision), enabled later rabbis to allow that it was permissible to remove obstacles to living if one was going to die anyway (thus, supporting Hananyah's actions).

Before the rabbis sought to codify proscriptions related to self-inflicted death, Second Temple exegetes sought to put a boundary up. As we have seen with martyrdom, the taking of one's life, was allowed under certain circumstances. Philo goes further, suggesting that the taking of the lives of family members was equally acceptable.

> We gladly put our throats at your disposal. Let them slaughter, butcher, carve our flesh without a blow struck or blood drawn by

---

106. Goldstein, 2 *Maccabees*, 492–93. See also Eisenberg, *JPS Guide*, 104; Moore, *Tobit*, 149.

107. See *Baba Kamma* 91b. See also *Genesis Rabbah: The Judaic Commentary on to the Book of Genesis*. See also *Genesis Rabbah* 34.13; Mekhilta *ba-hodesh* 8; Mishnah *Sanhedrin* 4.5.

108. As Droge has noted, Rabbinic literature is replete with tales of suicide, with some allowances. See Droge, "Suicide," 229.

109. Goldstein, *Suicide in Rabbinic Literature*, 26–29. See below in this section where this theme is expounded.

110. A reverse, of sorts, may be seen in the image of Jesus on the cross when the onlookers encourage Jesus to save himself. Like the early rabbis, the death of Jesus was seen as enacting obedience (Phil 2:8; Heb 5:8–9; 1 Pet 4:1–2).

us and do all the deeds that conquerors commit. But what need of an army! our selves will conduct the sacrifices, priests of a noble order:[111] wives will be brought to the altar by wife-slayers, brothers and sisters by fratricides, boys and girls in the innocence of their years by child-murderers. For the tragedian's vocabulary is needed for those who endure tragical misfortunes. Then standing in the midst of our kinsfolk after bathing ourselves in their blood, the right bathing for those who would go to Hades clean, we will mingle our blood with theirs by the crowning slaughter of ourselves. When we are dead let the prescript be carried out; not God himself could blame us who had a twofold motive, respectful fear of the emperor and loyalty to the consecrated laws. And this aim will be accomplished if we take our departure in contempt of the life which is no life.[112]

On the surface, this is easily suicide and murder. Underneath, it may be a form of martyrdom. Regardless, Philo—Paul's contemporary—understood the need in extreme circumstances to take a life without recrimination.

Beyond these rather easy examples are the *Tannaim*, first and second-century rabbis. In particular, Rabbi Ishmael gives us an example that is pertinent to our study.[113] For Rabbi Ishmael, prophets were routinely called to offer up their own lives on behalf of the Children of Israel. In fact, the Rabbi defends Jonah's exodus in such a way that it appears Jonah is challenging God whom the prophet is accusing (if only implicitly) of putting Israel in danger.

> A final, dissenting opinion defends Jonah by saying that the prophet fled his mission only because he had the welfare of the nation of Israel in mind; he was even willing to give up his own

111 Or "fine priests indeed"—a strange travesty of priesthood, καλοί being used ironically, as perhaps always when applied to persons.

112. Philo, *Legate*, 233–36.

113. B.Z. Wacholder raised the suggestion that the surviving work of the Rabbi is from the eighth century (Wacholder, "Date of the Mekilta," 117–44). Thus far, it is a suggestion and a minority one. I follow the early date as proposed by Lauterbach, *Mekilta de-Rabbi Ishmael*, xviii–xxvi. See also, Boyarin, "On the Status," 455–65; Porton, *Understanding Rabbinic Midrash*, 53–54. I note that E. P. Sanders makes use of Rabbi Ishmael's work, although with some caveat. He writes, "It is on the basis of this view that we take the bulk of the anonymous material in the Tannaitic midrashim to be an appropriate source for the study of Rabbinic Judaism in the last two-thirds of the second century CE. Some of the interpretations are doubtless traditional, but we have them as they passed through the schools of the second century" (Sanders, *Paul and Palestinian Judaism*, 69). See his full discussion in Sanders, *Paul and Palestinian Judaism*, 66–69.

life for Israel's sake (because he knew that God would capsize the ship if he tried to flee on it). And so, the section concludes, "you will find everywhere that the patriarchs and prophets," like Jonah, "offered [to give up] their lives on behalf of Israel."[114]

What was Jonah afraid of? That the Gentiles, in repenting, would in effect be condemning Israel.[115]

This same theme is picked up in the Ishmael's Midrash as the Rabbi discusses Exodus 15:2. Here, Ishmael is entertaining the idea that some mortal man could add glory to the Creator. The Rabbi then interprets this phrase to mean one who obeys the comments *and* is ready to die for the God of the Jews. He writes,

> For all the nations of the world ask Israel, saying: "What is thy beloved more than another beloved, that thou dost so adjure us" (Cant 5:9), that you are so ready to die for Him, and so ready to let yourselves be killed for Him?—For it is said: "Therefore do the maidens love Thee" (Cant 1:3), meaning, they love Thee unto death. And it is also written: "Nay but for Thy sake are we killed all the day" (Ps 44:23)—"You are handsome, you are mighty, come and intermingle with us."[116]

This continued refrain for being ready to die for God and on behalf of Israel, best exemplified by Jonah's intentional taking of the ship in order to be capsized, as a merit of devotion is not, at least in the Talmudic context, related to suicide and may even be said to be counter to it. However, it is necessary to note that those Jews writing near the time of the New Testament did not fail to see the virtue of a good man, or rather prophet, dying on behalf of Israel in order to protect Israel from God.

In turning to the Talmud, we find much the same allowance for voluntary death as we do in Rabbi Ishmael. During this period, Jewish martyrdom was given a place next to prayer and alms as a way to honor God, with the phrase *kiddush ha-Shem* rendered to them, almost as an epithet.[117] We see this develop in interpretations of particular passages. For example

114. Lauterbach, *Mekilta de-Rabbi Ishmael*, xv. Lauterbach notes that the contemporary context for such a statement is found in the destruction of the Second Temple, and helps to honor those Jews who had indeed died on behalf of Israel.

115. R. Ishmael used Jonah as a mirror image of Elijah. According to the rabbi, unlike Jeremiah and Jonah who concerned themselves with honor to both the Father and the son (i.e., Israel), Elijah was concerned only for God's honor. See, Fishbane, *Haftarot*, 134.

116. Lauterbach, *Mekilta de-Rabbi Ishmael*, 185.

117. Safrai, "Kiddush Hashem," 28–42. See also, Eisenberg, *JPS Guide*, 103.

as in the case of Samson, there is no condemnation of his last act—which is surely a self-inflicted death. Indeed, according to both the Babylonian and the Jerusalem versions, Rabbi Aha (c. third century) gave an increase to Samson's legend, noting that his *actual* last request was to request an eye for this world and one for the next.[118] This concern for the next world was primary in excluding suicide victims, but Samson's apocryphal request indicates—with rabbinic blessing—that his eternal course was set. Further, Rabbi Judah (c. second century) believed that in his act, Samson was able to cause the Philistines to still fear the deceased judge for another twenty years.[119] In both instances, Samson's self-inflicted death was seen as a being blessed by God and the rabbis.[120]

Because voluntary death did take place, elaborate systems were put in place that allowed for mourning, something especially mentioned by the Talmud as not allowed for someone who had intentionally taken their own life. We find such instances in the minor Talmudic tractate, אבל רבתי (*Semahot*). In this, specifically chapter 2, suicide is defined by the intention of the victim rather than act. The Rabbis go so far as to suggest that even those discovered strangled and hanging on a tree would not be counted a suicide—presumably because the intention could not be measured. It is not that the Rabbis did not attempt to measure the intention;[121] however, even when the intention was known there were caveats.[122] Beyond that, we have the motivation weighed as an allowance, such as in the case of Rabbi Ashi (c. fourth–fifth century) who brought about his own death by abstaining from food. His intention was to die, but his motivation was repentance.[123]

As S. Goldstein notes, whether it was Samson or the examples culled from rabbinic victims, the sole motivation was "intense piety."[124] For example, in *Abodah Zarah* 18a, the Jew is charged to harm (kill) himself rather

---

118. *Sotah* 1.8, I.3.

119. *Sotah* 1.8, I.9.B.

120. Goldstein notes that King Saul's death has become less a threat to suicide prohibitions. While not treated specifically within our timeframe, medieval commentators building on the Tannaim often made allowances—some based on predetermination—for Saul. See Goldstein, *Suicide*, 8–10.

121. For example, as they attempted to do in *Semahot* 2.2.

122. *Sem.* 2.4.

123. *Kiddushin* 81b.

124. Goldstein, *Suicide*, 28. See also Goldstein, *2 Maccabees*, 493. Goldstein cites *Lamentations Rabbah* and several Talmudic passages wherein suicide was allowed if the motivation was to preserve righteousness.

than worship idols.[125] Goldstein also notes that martyrdom was separated from self-inflicted death in nearly all ancient authorities.[126] In this, we find enough support that whether it was martyrdom, a form of self-inflicted death, or even a prophet attempting to die to prevent God from harming Israel, the Jews of the first few centuries found it an acceptable interpretation that one could in fact die by his own hand and still be declared righteous.

Excursus

In Matthew 12:39 (cf. Luke 11:30), Jesus in responding to the Pharisees' request for a sign berates them. He allows that only τὸ σημεῖον Ἰωνᾶ τοῦ προφήτου will be given to the generation. It is possible Rabbi Ishmael's interpretation did not owe to him an origin, but was an interpretation used by Jews looking for the Messiah for a generation or two before the destruction of the Temple—that Jonah attempted to cause his own death as a way to prevent God's dishonor of Israel.[127] This is Jonah's ultimate downfall, that he "cannot bring himself to believe that it is right for God to demonstrate that his mercy is more than the exclusive possession of the Jews."[128] Rather than becoming obedient, Jonah attempts to flee to a place where God cannot speak to the prophet. According to the ancient sage, this is Jonah's attempt at self-sacrifice.[129] By reexamining the Gospel passage in light of R. Ishmael, then, we find evidence of an expected Jewish *devotio*.

There is a cosmic crisis in Jonah (even without R. Ishmael's interpretation). YHWH has decided to cross divine territory and declare himself the supreme deity to the Ninevites. Further, this would demonstrate to Israel that their singular hold of God's law was about to end. The great legal court of the heavens was about to declare that Gentiles had to follow God's standards of righteousness. To any unsuspecting prophet, this may look to be

125. It is possible that this is a thought underlying the early Christian hymn found in Philippians 2:8.

126. Goldstein, *Suicide*, 42. There are exceptions to the rule, such as *Sanhedrin* 74a–b; however, it is these exceptions that give the rule strength.

127. This interpretation has been recognized by other scholars. See Keener, *New Testament*, Mt 12:38–41.

128. Gibson, *Temptations of Jesus*, 201. Gibson suggests R. Ishmael's interpretation Jonah hails from the first half of the first century.

129. Droge and Tabor notably disagree with R. Ishmael's (although they do not engage him) understanding of Jonah (Droge and Tabor, *Noble Death*, 60–61). They see the self-inflicted death as an attempt at "capital punishment for his rebellion against God."

the end of Israel as the Chosen People. Thus, Jonah chose to honor Israel and flee Israel's heavenly king and along the way, to freely offer himself as a sacrifice that would stave off the cosmic crisis.

In the Gospel passage, it is not merely the example of Jonah that is present, but also the Gentile Queen and her excursion to Solomon. In both instances, the books of the Jews reveal that the Gentiles in the story did come to accept the God of the Jews as their cosmic Lord (Jonah 3:1–10; Wis 6:1–11); however, the Gentiles only came to fidelity with God through particular figures of Israel—the prophet and the king. "They are indisputable evidence of two facts: first, of God's universal salvific concern; second, that God's saving purposes cannot be fully realized apart from Israel's cooperation."[130] Because of this, the faithful Gentiles will now stand on the Day of Judgment as witnesses *against* unfaithful Israel (Matt 12:42). Examining the mission of the Gospel's Jesus through the lens of R. Ishmael's interpretation of Jonah gives us a strong possibility that the sign Jesus spoke of is that of a prophet/king who will, on the behalf of Israel, offer his life to stave off a cosmic crisis.

What is the "σημεῖον?" Gibson offers the most compelling answer—Jesus himself:

> (A)s Son of Man Jesus must be to 'this generation' the same thing that Jonah was to the Ninevites. Now, as we have also seen, Jonah, according to the correlative, was an 'ensign' or 'standard.' But an 'ensign' or 'standard' of what? Given the thrust of the Jonah traditions, the answer, of course, is an 'ensign' or 'standard' of how boundless and all encompassing is God's love. So Jesus' justification for his giving no 'sign' but the 'sign' of Jonah' is, then, that in his words and actions he must be nothing less than what Jonah ultimately was to the Ninevites, *an embodiment of the mercy and graciousness of God*. This means that any 'sign' that Jesus might give would have to be compatible with what he himself embodied.[131]

To conclude, Jewish interpretations contemporaneously existing with Paul allowed for a prophet to find a way to die in order to avert a cosmic crisis. Jonah was the most proffered one and because of this, we can understand the Jesus of Matthew and Luke as speaking of himself who will offer himself as a sacrifice in order to bring to an end the cosmic crisis separating Jew and Gentile—if not the cosmic crisis separating God and Jew.

130. Gibson, *Temptations of Jesus*, 204.

131. Gibson, *Temptations of Jesus*, 208.

CONCLUSION

Can the interpretation of Jesus' execution by Paul to the Galatians have a genesis in Early Judaism? According to Sam K. Williams, one cannot see a Jewish origin for the image of the death of Jesus as a self-sacrificial beneficial death.[132] For him "the concept of Jesus' death as saving event had as its creative source a tradition of beneficial, effective human death for others ... this concept originated among Christians who not only spoke Greek but were also thoroughly at home in the Greek-Hellenistic thought world."[133] Elisabeth Schüssler Fiorenza supports this notion as well, writing, "the interpretation of Jesus' death as atonement for sins is much later than is generally assumed in New Testament scholarship. The notion of atoning sacrifice does not express the Jesus movement's understanding and experience of God but is a later interpretation of the violent death of Jesus in cultic terms.... The Death of Jesus was not a sacrifice and was not demanded by God but brought about by the Romans."[134] Given what we have seen, it is impossible to not locate the death of Jesus in Jewish theological speculation of the time.

The Jewish books and post-biblical writings tackle the topic of self-inflicted death. What we can see are patterns similar to that of the Romans, so much so that even without the Latin labels, *devotio,* martyrdom, and self-inflicted deaths are easily seen among the Jews. Further, there exists a mixture of cosmic crisis and even to some—small—level a presence of the divinization of the victim. Perhaps this seemingly impossible reality where the violent end of Jesus is rooted in both Early Judaism *and* Roman mythology is allowed because the only neatly drawn lines between Jew and Roman are those crafted in modern histories rather than in the cosmopolitan and syncretic times of the ancient world. We cannot forget the examples of Samson and Jonah in our discussion here. The Jewish Paul writing to an audience of Jews and Gentiles in provincial Rome would not have lacked sufficient Jewish authorities to interpret the death of Jesus as

132. Williams is not the only one, as many across the centuries have struggled to understand how the ignoble crucifixion of a convicted state traitor would come to represent victory and libertas. Some suggest separating the Jesus who wanted to die from the so-called Historical Jesus (Droge and Tabor, *Noble Death,* 116–17). This present study will resolve that question. We will return to the concept seemingly self-contradictory "beneficial death" of Jesus in the conclusion of this work.

133. Williams, *Jesus' Death as Saving Event,* 230.

134. Schüssler Fiorenza, *In Memory of Her,* 130.

a very human Jew, who knowing of a cosmic crisis as well as knowing of his own divinity, freely forced his own death so that he may bring about something new.[135] However, since the very Jewish Paul also was Roman and speaking to Roman Gentiles, we can look to the Romans for added weight to our hypothesis.

135. The contradiction between "very human" and divinity becomes clear in the discussion of Cato the Younger in chapter 4 and is a necessary play on words.

Chapter 4

The Roman Devotio

INTRODUCTION

IN THIS CHAPTER, I will explore several examples of *devotio* with the goal of defining the specific model required for reading the death of Jesus, rather than a martyrdom, as that of a *devotio*. There are two recognized models of *devotio* we will use as a catalyst for understanding and imaging the Roman model that may give us a framework for reading the death of Jesus, not only in Galatians but also throughout the New Testament. These models are of the religious-political mixing required by the epoch we are discussing. After discussing the recent work on *devotio*, I will turn to presenting the examples of *devotio*. These are Decius Mus, Spurius Postumius, Cato the Younger, and the Emperor Otho along with Seneca's *Hercules Oetaeus*.

ROMAN SELF-DEATH

It is necessary to briefly discuss Roman models akin to those discussed in the previous chapter. In chapter 3, I presented a list of examples drawn from Jewish sources as evidence that during the time of Paul, it would have been acceptable—even seen as a righteous act—for someone to suffer a self-inflicted death, even to the point of having that death offered as a *human* sacrifice to God, although this view was changing (see the section on the Rabbinic reaction). While the Jews did not have any formulated or well-entrenched cultural models for someone we could see as an example of an exclusively Jewish *devotio*, nevertheless what exists is enough to suggest that while Paul may have more easily used the Roman model in describing the necessary and atoning death of Jesus on the cross, he could have less easily done so with a Jewish prototype.

Paul is speaking to a group of people with their own model, notably, the Roman standard. Because of this, I will now turn to exploring the Roman models of self-inflicted death in order to show such a thing was commonplace enough that Jesus' suicide would not have stood out as anything remarkably unexpected. What makes his death different, Paul would argue, is the efficacy of the sacrifice—an efficacy only possible through the *devotio*. Further, even if Paul had not intended to draw such sharp parallels between the death of Jesus and the Roman *devotio* in his emplotment recasting, the story of the crucifixion would have naturally appealed to a Roman audience exactly because it carried so many hallmarks of the *devotio*. Rather than a passive similarity, this aggressive appeal is exactly what we find—and perhaps would expect to find—in Paul's letter to the Galatians.

While the linguistic nuance was briefly and variedly discussed in the previous chapter, exactly because we are moving into the Greco-Roman world where such precise terms were often ritualized, we must briefly explore the various terms employed for those who take their own life. There is no single Latin equivalent for the seventeenth-century English creation of "suicide." Rather, as the Greeks and Romans were apt to do, there is a certain poetic turn of phrase used in extant literature. The Greeks had *lambano thanaton* (to grasp death), *teleutao bion* (to end life), *hekousios apothneisko* (to die voluntarily) and *autothanatos* (dying by oneself). Likewise, the Latins had *ambitiosa mors* (ambitious death), *mors voluntaria* (voluntary death), and *manus sibi inferre* (to bring one's hand against oneself).[1] This myriad of uses, as well as the focus on one particular model, makes it necessary to limit this volume to just a few examples in order to show that unlike the Jews, the Romans did have certain expectations (rather than allowances) of those who chose to die by their own hand.

---

1. For a more thorough discussion on the linguistic buffet, see Droge and Tabor, *Noble Death*, 6–7.

Suicide in Roman Thought

The Romans had a long tradition of suicide, so much so that it had become engrained in their national identity. As E. R. Dodds states, "In these centuries a good many persons were consciously or unconsciously in love with death."[2] Roman suicide, like most things Roman, found its genesis among the Greeks. Plato's work, *Phaedo*, contributed greatly the Stoic view, among other schools as well, of suicide as the final mastery of fate. Plato borrows Socrates's words to suggest that death, because of the promise of a reward on the other side, is preferred and urged his students to follow him quickly.[3] Granted, he refused to offer a chance for his disciples to take their own life, as this was strictly forbidden. After arguing over his moral clause, Socrates proposes a solution. Rather than taking one's life freely and simply to join ranks with the living who have died, he demands a necessity. If a necessity to take one's life is found, then it is no longer immoral.[4] Perhaps this is why so many Stoics would find themselves with such a great necessity, even to the point of interpreting the breaking of a finger or the stubbing of a toe as the call of a god to die.[5]

While Plato's *Phaedo* does make an appearance later in this work, more important to our present study is Seneca's *Epistle 70*. Here, he writes to laud suicide if it entails political freedom. He ends the epistle with the solemn, almost horrific announcement, "Reason advises us to die, if we may, according to our own style and if this cannot be, she advises us to die according to our own ability, to take whatever we will to do violence to ourselves. It is criminal to live as a thief, but on the other hand, it is most noble to do so."[6] Seneca would go on to commit suicide after the failure of a conspiracy to kill Nero, who himself later fell on his own sword.

Suicide was such a commonplace sight in Rome it gave rise to a concept, *Romana mors*, complete with images of dramatic suicides serving as the evening's entertainment. The act of taking one's own life became almost a standard norm but it was not associated with depression. Rather that the stark contrast offered by depression or a joy to die, the reality was more

---

2. Dodds, *Pagan and Christian*, 135.

3. Plato, *Phaedo*, 61bc, 64.

4. Plato, *Phaedo*, 62c.

5. Thus is the story of Zeno, the founder of Stoicism. See Diogenes Laertius, *Lives of the Philosophers*, 7.28.

6. Seneca, *Ep* 70.28; *Ad Lucilium Epistulae Morales*, 73.

often an overreaction to events. Romans took their own life due to certain "signs," losses in war, even criminal charges. Added to this is the developed ritual and even stylistic etiquette Romans used. At one point, suicides become a public event, a transformation prompting parodies at Nero's court.[7]

It must be stressed that a canyon of cultural context separates the connection between the Roman suicide and Jewish suicide. It suffices us to simply point out that in both cultures relevant to the authors of the New Testament, suicide was allowed at least for particular instances, especially to avoid loss and to prevent humiliation. Neither of these instances sufficiently describes the death of Jesus, for reasons I will detail later in this study.

Martyrdom in Roman Thought

For our study, I want to focus on a few examples of what could be considered martyrdom in the (Greco-)Roman world. The first illustration is from the *Funeral Oration*, a work performed by Demosthenes to eulogize the soldiers of Philip II.[8] In this case, Demosthenes commends the heroic sacrifice by Erechteus of his daughters to stave off the attack of Athens. Our orator gave this speech to qualify the deaths of the Macedonians and to remind the citizens that such sacrifice was sometimes needful. The style and manner of this death, in the line of battle and for the fatherland, is something the citizens replicated for centuries.[9] While it does not suggest religious martyrdom, this example does allow for the sacrifice of one's life, or the life of another, to preserve some sort of belief system.

If we examine the life and death of ancient philosophers we find tales of harrowing deaths and suicides to preserve one school or another. Perhaps they could have escaped death, but as Xenophon reminds by giving his own teacher as the example, they chose to die on principle. Finally, there is the story of Lucretia who was, after her husband had won a wager, raped. By her hand she stabbed her heart and declared her innocence. Indeed, her self-death is seen as a sign of her innocence and as such, her body was displayed as a sign of rebellion against the oppressors. Unlike suicide, both Socrates and Lucretia die *for something*.

7. For more on the suicide cult at Rome, see Hill, *Ambitiosa Mors*.

8. Euripides, *Iphigenia at Aulis* 1374–99. Translation adapted from Diggle, *Euripidis Fabulae*.

9. See Moss, *Myth of Persecution*, 35.

Whereas it may be easy to suppose the difference between suicide and martyrdom is an outside force, i.e., a second party killing someone, it is not such an easy demarcation. After all, suicide can be accomplished by forcing another person into action against the victim as we see in several examples from the Jewish Scriptures. There may be an almost unintelligible thin line separating martyrdom and suicide; however, there is much nuance to that line. Martyrdom requires the person dying to be given a choice to live. In suicide, the only goal is death.

Human Sacrifice in Roman Thought

In the Roman world, the province of Galatia had at least one cult practicing human sacrifice near the time of Jesus. "Chieftains were notorious for Druid-style ritualized human sacrifice, a practice similar to that noted by Julius Caesar among the Celts in Gaul."[10] Rome proper had come to recognize the act of sacrificing humans as something completely foreign, but we must separate this from ritual killing. This latter instance, the *devotio*, while it varied in practice and purpose, amounts to self-sacrifice. Further, there is the matter of the burying alive two Greeks and two Gauls, something that still troubled Plutarch centuries later. Finally, "to accuse someone at Rome of having sacrificed a person rather than an animal was to accuse them of having broken all norms or proper civilized *Roman* behaviour."[11] As with both suicide and martyrdom before, human sacrifice was allowed if it met certain criteria.

While caveats for taking a life without cause were made in both the Jewish and Roman world, the qualifications decreased nearer the Semitic line of religious ethics one came. Suicide for the sake of suicide was condemned. Indeed, even in Jewish allowances for a necessitated suicide, the act was upheld as a crime but the motivations examined to determine blameworthiness. The rabbis likewise viewed martyrdom harshly. Finally, human sacrifice was profusely forbidden with great apologetic strides taken to allow for the attempted sacrifice of Isaac. We must stress the fact that suicide, martyrdom, and human sacrifice was neither the normal behavior of either the Jew or the Roman and most likely would have been interpreted as something unholy—unless the intent and culpability of the victim was deemed sufficiently worthy. With these comments too briefly examined,

10. Harrill, "Asia Minor," 135.

11. Beard et al., *Religions of Rome*, 156–60.

I will now turn to the crux of this volume, the Roman *devotio*, an event incorporating all three—suicide, martyrdom, and human self-sacrifice.

THE TWO MODELS OF DEVOTIO

H. S. Versnel has proposed what have become the standard categories for *devotio*. He separates *devotio* into two types, the *devotio hostium* and the *devotio ducis*. In the former, the victim was the enemy, dedicated to the gods, while the latter, the victim is the general.[12] In another essay, Versnel examines the death of Jesus, albeit from a rather wide angle instead of particular passages, via various definitions of "noble death" exhumed from pagan sources.[13] He maintains his earlier stance on the *devotio*, limiting it to two, but does not connect the crucifixion to either Decius or Cato and the models they represent, mentioning this figures almost in passing. In this brief section, I will examine Versnel's definitions before moving on to examples of why not all death of heroes neatly fall into the model of *devotio ducis*.

In each paradigm, the death of the victim is linked to an overarching goal; namely, victory. While one model involved self-sacrifice, the other involved the sacrifice of someone, or something, else. Thus, the separation lies in the object of the vow, not so much the intended result. For the first model, Versnal quotes Livy 8.9 (we will return to this below in more detail) and Macrobius's *Saturnalia*. In Livy, the Roman General Decius Mus extends himself as the object of the vow although he does so while crashing through the ranks of the enemy. It may be tempting to unite the two over Decius's body, although it was never found; however, Decius's only vow was for himself.

Each *devotio* is indeed a religious ritual.[14] Yet, while Versnal allows this distinction, he insists the real distinction lies between *consecratio* and *votum*. Both remain legal, religious, and based on free will of some sort. As Versnal points out, while quoting W. W. Fowler, the former is a conditional promise with the gods able to act, or react, with a set pattern within

---

12. See Versnel, "Two Types," 365–410.

13. See also Versnel, "Making Sense of Jesus' Death," 213–94.

14. See Deubner, *Die Devotion der Decier*; Fugier, *Recherches sur l'expression*, 45–57; Arnold, *Les sacrifices humains*, 27–36; Stübler, *Die Religiosität des Livius*, 172–205; Schilling, "Roman Religion," 474.

previously agreed upon arrangements.[15] The *consecratio* occurred before the expected promise by choice of the immolated, thus forcing the gods to act. Finally, every *votum* requires the *consecratio* while *consecratio* does not require any such vow.

Perhaps the most infamous of the *devotio hostium* is the leveling of Carthage by Roman force, as related by Macrobius in *Saturnalia* 3.9–10. In this instance, the city was scorched not to appease the gods but to fulfill a vow wherein if Rome was victorious one of the enemy's cities would be given to the gods. Versnal calls this a "true *votum*" because it includes all of the needed elements, namely the vow and the action of the gods in granting Roman victory. Further, there is the transaction between the gods and the Romans, not only granting victory but in securing the salvation of the *vovens*.[16] In a real sense, the *votum* in the *devotio hostium* is redeemed only by the *consecratio*, although not a self-sacrifice. It is neither the victory itself nor the discharge of the city, but the death of the enemies bringing something of a completion to the entire ordeal. While this is not necessarily human sacrifice, there is a promise contained herein that if victory is granted, there will be death and lots of it.

There are two final elements the ancient historiographers call to our attention. The first is the curse laid upon Carthage as part of the *votum*.[17] The *defixio* (κατάδεσμος), a part of the *devotio*, is not the sum total of the ritual.[18] Rather, unlike the *devotio* where the agreeing parties know of the conditions, the *defixio* is placed upon an unaware party, namely, the *vicarios*.[19] Whereas the *devotio* is seen as a positive intention, the intention of the *defixio* is one of destruction.[20] The curse to Carthage, then, is a result of the *devotio* but not the *devotio* itself. Simply, as the word *devotio* itself is made

---

15. Versnal, "Two Types," 367–69. See, Fowler, *Religious Experience*, 200.

16. Versnal, "Two Types," 378.

17. Along with Carthage as one of the cities given in the *devotio hostium*, another, more familiar and relevant city is recorded by Macrobius has having suffered a curse. In 146 BCE, Corinth was cursed. This record survives only in the literary record and the historical fact of it has been challenged in recent scholarship. See Friesen et al., *Corinth in Contrast*, 21.

18. Other distinctions include the use of magic, the lack of free will by at least one of the parties, and the intent.

19. Versnal, "Two Types," 388–94.

20. Audollent, "Devotio ou Defixio?" 37; *Defixionum Tabellae*, xxxviff; cf. the recent survey in Preisendanz, "Fluchtafel," 1–29.

of other parts, such as *de-* and *vot-*, the act includes several moving pieces and no single one of them should be thought of as the sum of the whole.

The second element, as mentioned above, is the *vicarios*.[21] The *vicarios* is the substitute sacrifice. For instance, in the case of Rome and Carthage, whereby the last city was committed to the *devotio* for the sake of the gods, it was not for one person but for the whole of the Roman people. Likewise, Versnal follows others in giving examples various substitution sacrifices in which something was killed for the life of another. Rarely, except in cases of war, were humans sacrificed although humans dying in close temporal proximity to the miraculous recovery of another can be claimed to be a sacrifice such as in the case of Aelius Aristides.[22] In this instance, the orator recovers from a fatal disease after someone else dies. He lays credit at the feet of the gods who have given him that man's life for his own.[23] More generally, animals were sacrificed as a substituted offering.[24] Indeed, the role of the *vicarios* led Versnal to suggest the *devotio hostium* is the older of the two rites.

We have already seen the mixing of ideas between the Latin and the Semitic peoples. We should not seek to understand Paul, or the New Testament, solely in the Jewish world; therefore, as below with the *devotio decius*, I will now give examples from Jewish sources (since by virtue of discussing the Roman idea Roman sources were given) of what may be described as *devotio hostium*. For the purpose of brevity, I will limit it to canonical Jewish sources. I will examine only those examples wherein someone was

21. Carcopino suggests the etymology of the Latin word is actually Semitic, "Or, à ce mot do vicarius semble être attachée, dans la langue religieuse latine, une valeur propre, liée naturellement à la notion de l'être dont le sacrifice épargne, en le rachetant, celui d'un autre," (Carcopino, "Survivances par substitution," 44). For a Phoenician connection to Vergil's Dido, see Grottaneli, "I connotai fenici," 319–27; Thompson, *Penitence and Sacrifice*, wherein the information from Curtiss is derived.

22. Aristides, *Hieroi Logos* 2.44.

23. Another example along this line is the case of Cassius Philippus, who upon arriving on Sardinia, nearly succumbed to a life-threatening disease. His wife's death is given credit as saving Cassius's live. See Bouchier, *Sardinia in Ancient Times*; Chaniotis et al., "Karales."

24. This is immediately recognizable as the act of "scapegoating." While the English label comes from the Jewish concept, we cannot forget the use of it, even if by another name (*caput*), among the Romans. In this, the evil given by the gods is transferred to something else, notably an animal. See Maximus, *Factorum et Dictorum*, 2:4–5, as a contemporary example as well as Versnal, "Two Types," 393n79.

exchanged for the place of another to belay wrath (without clearly defining terms).

With these closer perimeters, there are only a few instances where one object (i.e., city, nation, or other) was substituted for Israel. The first is found in Isaiah 43:3–4 when YHWH recalls the exodus by saying he had given Egypt, Nubia, and Seba as the price for Israel's freedom. If this was not enough, YHWH was more than willing to exchange Assyria and Edom for his people's liberty. This passage should likewise inform our opinion of Isaiah 51:9–11 with its own allusions to the crossing of the dried seabed, but in this case, what is given for Israel's safety is an ancient deity. Death and destruction is involved and in the case of Egypt, a long series of curses.[25] To add to this are the images of substitution found in Numbers 3:40–51 where one tribe was substituted for the other tribes as an offering to God. Likewise, Exodus 30:11–16 has the substitution of shekels (a form of sacrifice) for the life of the Israelites.[26] Elihu reminds Job angels can similarly bring a price to redeem those in the pit (Job 33:23–25).

The act of giving a child (or to use biblical language, causing a child to be passed through the fires) is not foreign to the Hebrew canon, even if the majority of mentions is condemnation. I call attention to several examples. One of the more infamous examples in the Hebrew bible is that of Jephthah who vows, "If you will deliver the Ammonites into my hands, then the first creature that comes out of the door of my house to meet me when I return from them safely shall be the Lord's; I shall offer that as a whole-offering" (Judg 11:30–31, REB). The warrior defeats the Ammonites and returns home to find his daughter rushing out to greet him. Likewise, in 2 Kings 3:26–27 the king of Moab offered his own son for victory over Israel. It was not rewarded.[27]

4Q251, fragment 13, may serve as an example as well:

1 [. . . on]e another [. . .]
2 [. . . under] the tree, to the unclean [. . .]
3 [. . . when one finds] a wounded man who has fallen in [. . .]

---

25. See Ezekiel 32 and Isaiah 19, not to mention the oft-remembered plagues laidout upon Egypt including the death of the first-born.

26. The language in Exodus 30:11–16 may be important in the development of Pauline language, specifically the use of λύτρον in 30:16 LXX.

27. The King of Moab was not along in using his son as a sacrifice. Several kings of Israel were said to do the same. David offered the sacrifice of Saul's lineage to end the famine (2 Sam 21); Ahab built Jericho by first sacrificing his son (1 Kgs 16:33; cf. Josh 6:26–27); and Manasseh as well (2 Kgs 21:6).

4 [. . . and they shall break there the heif]er's [neck] in [the ravi]ne
in return for (his) life [. . .]
5 [. . .] it is a substitution; everyone who has been brought to death
[. . .]
6 [. . .] everyone who has no life inside is dead, in a gr[ave].[28]

The fragment is embedded in a section listing sins and prohibitions, but it is the only one to speak about an offering in the place of something else. Whereas other offerings can be made, in the case of a loss of life, the bull must be slaughtered as a way of maintaining peace. Fragment 13 is close to Exodus 21:29, although in the canonical source, the bull and the owner will be put to death as a penalty for inaction rather than as a return for a life.[29]

What these examples have in common rest almost squarely on the notion that one object (person, animal, or even a city) is given in the place of another *without* its consent. Whereas Rome gave Carthage to its gods, without the blessing of the people of the city, YHWH could give Egypt, Nubia, and Seba for the liberty and freedom of Israel. When it comes to human sacrifice, what we have recorded is not as an appeasement to sin or breaching the covenant with the gods, or YHWH as in the case of Israel, but in exchange for something else, rather victory in battle or perhaps a simple prayer.[30] While the Jews and other Semitic peoples would not have called their sacrifice by the Latin word, there are striking similarities.

---

28. Martínez and Tigchelaar, "Dead Sea Scrolls," 501.

29. I am pointedly forgoing the inclusion of Leviticus 16 for a several reasons. First, it may cloud the subject matter. While animals can be sacrificed, the scapegoat was not. It was merely left to wander into the wilderness carrying the sins of the people with it. Second, while sins (roughly defined) may be part of the *devotio hostium*, more often it was not. Simply, this form of the *devotio* was about trading one thing for another. The life and freedom of Carthage was traded for Rome's vivacity and liberty. The firstborn of Egypt was traded for the freedom of YHWH's "firstborn." Sins simply are not a factor. Finally, while there are some suggestions that Carthage was re-sacrificed, it is not a continuing ritual, unlike Yom Kippur. While the annual Passover celebration remembered the giving of Egypt, it did not reenact it. Simply, Leviticus 16 falls outside the realm of *devotio hostium*.

30. For examples of child sacrifice at Carthage, see Xella et al., "Phoenician Bones of Contention," 1199–207.

EXAMPLES OF ROMAN **DEVOTIO**

What follows is a list of examples showcasing, rather than explaining, the *devotio*.[31] I find this helpful in showing that the practice, rather than a name or category or other speculated rules, is prevalent in Paul's world. While some of these examples fall outside of Paul's time, what I hope becomes apparent is that there were rules and expectations, as well as inherent meaning to the act. While Paul may not call it a *devotio*, what he would have known as a Roman educated citizen are the examples of those in the Roman world. I would again note the discussion in chapter one regarding emplotments. It is not necessary to name something easily identified by practice. Throughout, I call attention to specific details, such as the cosmological crisis and the divinity of the victim that will only help us read the death of Jesus in Galatians more true to Paul's cognitive environment.

Marcus Curtius

Roman General Decius Mus (c. 340 BCE) performed by far the most famous *devotio* from which all other examples are given. Before him, however, is the mythic Marcus Curtius (c. 370 BCE). Livy recounts an earthquake or "the action of some other force" that destroyed the governmental center of Rome. Everyone attempted to work to refill the chasm, but in the end, it was pointless. Only when the gods suggest the priests, the fetials, inquire of them did the Romans turn to the passive deities for help. They required a sacrifice "on that spot" of the most precious item in their possession "if men wished the Roman republic to be eternal." Curtius discovered the answer to the riddle, that of the valor of the native sons. He then "devoted himself to the gods below. Then mounting his horse, which had been caparisoned as magnificently as possible, he leaped in full armour into the cavern."[32]

Decius Mus

Unlike his account of Curtius, Livy is able to draw on what he considers solid history in describing the self-sacrifice of Decius Mus. In the finality

---

31. There may be time to better separate the categories Versnel has given us, highlighting examples like Cato. For now, this present study will not challenge their brevity, which is why I find it necessary to give examples.

32. Livy, *History of Rome* 7.5.3–7.

of the battle between the Roman allies against the Latins, Decius Mus gave a speech employing the gods of his people to take his sacrifice and ensure his army not only survives but also triumphs. After the speech, the Roman Consul dons his ceremonial wardrobe tied in the fashion of a sacrificial animal, and dashes off into the midst of the other army, thereby forcing his death.[33] Livy then records, "He was observed by both armies to present a more majestic appearance than human, as one sent from heaven as an expiation (*piaculum*) of all the wrath of the gods, to transfer to the enemy destruction turned away from his own side."[34]

The language of the speech as well as of Livy's record of the reaction is one of justice, hence the language of *piaculum*. Nicole Belayche notes, "Religious relationships were defined as an engagement between two partners, the *uotum*, for they were first rooted in justice, and not in affective links with the gods, even if such a contractual approach did not prevent feelings."[35] By doing so publicly, Belayche assures us, Decius Mus did not intend to invoke any magical realms but only to offer a vow.[36] By offering himself, Decius Mus offered the expiation for the crime of war.[37] By offering his enemy through his own blood, the general removed the crime of war. DeMaris rightly points out that is what makes Decius's *devotio* a curative rite.[38]

DeMaris gives five elements of such a rite. The first is "a threat to the community." The fledgling Roman Republic is engaged in a war it is likely to lose. Already, one Consul member had executed his son because of a lack of discipline. Previous sacrifices had proved unhelpful. Small skirmishes showed the weakness in the Roman position. Thus, Decius called for the priest to tell him what to do. This meets DeMaris's second element, "the designation of a community member in response, who undergoes status

33. Specifically, Decius was said to have tied his toga into the Gabine knot, a method used in ritual sacrifice of animals. This was done according to the Roman pontiff's instructions. See Dubourdieu, "Cinctus Gabinus," 3–20. In Book X, Livy recounts the story of the son of Decius Mus, likewise named, who argues that his father, because he could make a religious vow, was also acceptable to the fetial priesthood. See Oakley, *Commentary on Livy*, 96. The younger Decius is said to have likewise committed the *devotio*.

34. Livy, *History of Rome* 8.9.10.

35. Belyache, "Religious Actors in Daily Life," 280–81.

36. Beylache, "Religious Actors in Daily Life," 287–88.

37. For more on the atonement latent in Livy's recounting of Decius Mus, see Avemarie and van Henten, *Martyrdom and Noble Death*, 20–21.

38. DeMaris, *Ritual World*, 101–3.

transformation over the course of the rite," the more so when it is given to Decius to become the ultimate sacrifice. More than this, however, is the transfiguration of the General before the assembled crowd in which he came to appear greater than any human.[39] The "ritual action that concentrates and directs divine power" is Decius's Gabine knot. His rushing headlong into the enemy ranks completed the fourth element. Finally, in the realm of expectation, the fifth element requires that the sacrifice succeed. History records well the victory over the Latins by the Roman forces and the eventual empire.[40]

Decius made an impact in early Christianity. Tertullian, writing in the second century, notes, "witness the devotion of the Decii, ratified by Heaven; and witness too Curtius and the gulf, whose yawning mouth horse and rider, or the honour due to their devotion, closed."[41] Lactantius, writing between 303 and 311, cites the same examples in his *Institutes 3.12.* This latter author is notable given his help in supporting Augustine in prohibiting self-death.

Spurius Postumius

History affords a rather more pleasant ending to Spurius Postumius (c. 321 BCE) than it does Decius. After a brief war with the Samnites, Postumius, seeing Rome's eventual defeat, offers a convention. In this, he and the Tribunes, among others, would return to Rome to first surrender their titles and then to the Samnites as a form of humiliation. The Senate first balked at the treaty, but after an impassioned speech, Livy records, "Both the speech and the speaker produced a great impression on all who heard him, including the tribunes, who were so far influenced by what they had heard that they formally placed themselves at the disposal of the senate. They immediately resigned their office and were handed over to the fetials to be conducted with the rest to Caudium."[42] Postumius had saved the entire Roman army by promising his public humiliation. Further, in his speech he

---

39. As Avemarie and van Henten note, "Decius has become a sacred person, belonging to the realm of the gods and that of the dead, although he still has to complete his mission" (Avemarie and van Henten, *Marytrdom and Noble Death*, 38n119).

40. DeMaris, *Ritual World*, 103.

41. Tertullian and Minucius Felix, *Tertullian's Apology and de Spectaculis*, 331.

42. Livy, *History of Rome 9.10.1–2.*

urges the Senate to consider his surrender as transference. Instead of Rome and the gods of Rome surrendering, it was the General.[43]

Livy, again, records the reaction. "The name of Postumius was in all men's mouths, he was extolled to the skies, his conduct was put on a level with the selfsacrifice of P. Decius and other splendid deeds of heroism. It was through his counsel and assistance, men said, that the State had found its way out of a dishonourable and guilty peace; he was exposing himself to the rage of the enemy and all the tortures they could inflict as an expiatory victim for the Roman people."[44] The death was eventually forestalled as the Roman general who was to surrender Postumius instead attacked the unsuspecting and war-weary Samnites. However, the account is still a *devotio* as it involves self-sacrifice to avoid defeat, albeit the self-sacrifice became limited only to humiliation that was resurrected into hero status for Postumius.[45]

The role of the gods and the social order in Postumius's story, however, is of peculiar note. After Rome was made aware of the army's defeat at the hands of the Samnites, civil upheaval threatened. Livy records reaction to the generals and the army as one of umbrage. "Their indignation was not confined to the generals or the officers who had made the convention, even the innocent soldiers were the objects of resentment, they said they would not admit them into the City."[46] The soldiers would slowly enter the city at night and hide in their homes, afraid of what the citizens would do. The Consuls likewise did the same. The first real government action Rome enjoyed was Postumius's negotiated surrender. Society was, in effect, crumbling with the very existence of the Republic at stake.

The religious elements are likewise seen. In 9.9.10, Postumius explains the defeat was an accident on both sides, "The gods deprived both the enemy's commanders and your own of their senses." The scene of the supposed surrender was enacted as a sacrifice complete with the Roman fetials who administered the stripping away of the victims clothing and their binding and gave the benediction, "I do herewith make surrender to you of these men, to the end that the Roman people may he absolved from the guilt of

43. Livy, *History of Rome* 9.96.

44. Livy, *History of Rome* 9.10.3–4.

45. We must understand this in the same vein as Decius Mus given Livy's own suggestion that Postumius is afforded the high honors given to Decius Mus.

46. Livy, *History of Rome* 9.7.9.

a heinous and detestable act."[47] Indeed, the gods play a passive role, but the sacrifice is still made to them, even if it is not about a collection of souls or blood. Rather, the *devotio* of Spurius Postumius was about the guilt of loss and war and as a substitution for the city of Rome itself.[48]

Seneca's Tragedy of Evil

Before we arrive at our final two examples, we must examine Seneca's *Hercules Oetaeus*, a Roman reinterpretation of the Greek myth.[49] This will serve as a bridge to the story of Cato the Younger, given that it is Seneca's nephew, Lucan, who supplies us with the most detailed view of *devotio*. The examination of a literary *devotio* is not meant to take away the historicity of the death of Jesus but to better inform the literary developments in the view, especially the Stoic view, of a self-sacrifice.

Seneca changed the Greek form of tragedy, from that of fate to that of evil.[50] This fits the rather Stoic view of controlling fate as the hero of the story knows full well his end but chooses to meet it, regardless of the costs. As Charles Segal notes, the main character suffers "guilt, take(s) responsibility for their death by their own uncontrolled emotions, and suffer(s) the physical and moral consequences of their actions."[51] Much of the violent elements of the story are internalized in the characters, however. Because of this, the hero is often separated from that which makes him human, including the outside world. The character suffers privately, but in a public manner. We see this exemplified in Seneca as well as his nephew Lucan.

There are several elements that must be drawn out of *Hercules Oetaeus*. The poem begins with Hercules speaking to his father, Jupiter, decrying the closing of heaven and the need, then, for the son to act as the father on earth.[52] Hercules is not the only forsaken object in the poem, as later we

47. Livy, *History of Rome* 9.10.9.

48. This ritual is different than the scapegoat analogy often applied to ancient sacrifice cults. See Bremmer, "Scapegoat Rituals in Ancient Greece," 299–320.

49. Seneca's authorship of this tragedy is in question. For now, I will side with the suggestion the orator did write this work. Harrison, "Claudian Castores," 124–27.

50. See Opelt, "Senecas Konzeption des Tragischen," 92–128, esp. 93.

51. Segal, "Boundary Violation," 140.

52. Seneca, *Hercules Oetaeus*, 1–12. It must be noted that Hercules, at least in Seneca's description, is not a demigod, but a mortal who desires to become a god. See Harrisons, "Themes," 638. An early Church writer recognizes Hercules was fully human but somehow divested himself of such limitations. See *Quod idola dii non sint*, 2.

come to understand all of earth is as well.[53] His death is chosen by himself and with the understanding it has been prophesied and is a needful act to give him the divine status he cherishes. "We complain no more; such end was meet, that no living thing might conquer Hercules. Now let me choose a death glorious, renowned, illustrious, full worthy of myself."[54] This is not merely about a suicide to claim some inheritance, but about vengeance upon the gods that had thus far forsaken him. Hercules had said as much in Seneca's prequel of sorts, *Hercules Furens*.[55] In doing so, in claiming the ability to decide for himself how he would finally approach that which Fate had laid out for him, Hercules decided to destroy the groves of the gods as a final act of revenge. The funeral pyre that engulfs Hercules likewise consumes the sacred hill of the gods while turning Hercules into a divinity sans the mortal body.[56]

Finally, the death of Hercules is quite simply the end of the world. Seneca, writing in a Stoic cosmological setting, would see the signs of distress as emblematic of the stretching of the world's bonds to their breaking points. Hercules, says, "*nunc, pater, caecum chaos redid decebat, hinc et hinc compagibus ruptis uterque debuit frangi polus.*"[57] He appeals to Jupiter as his father not to let the poles ordering the universe to be destroyed. We must set this phrase within the whole of the passage that reads,

> Conuerte, Titan clare, anhelantes equos,
> emitte noctem: pereat hic mundo dies
> quo morior, atra nube inhorrescat polus;
> obsta nouercae. nunc, pater, caecum chaos
> reddi decebat, hinc et hinc compagibus
>
> ruptis uterque debuit frangi polus;
> quid parcis astris? Herculem amittis, pater.[58]

---

53. Seneca, *Hercules Oetaeus*, 1587.

54. Seneca, *Hercules Oetaeus*, 1472.

55. Seneca, *Hercules Furens*, 1240–46, 1301–10.

56. Ovid records the death and transformation much like Livy does for Decius Mus, that of an august transformation. The poet declares, "*parte sui meliore viget, maiorque videri coepit et augusta fieri gravitate verendus*" (Ovid, *Met.* 9.269–70). It was debated among ancient authors as to what was left behind and how Hercules as made a god. Briefly, Hercules left fully the moral coil upon the pyre, burned like the oak grove.

57. Seneca, *Hercules Oetaeus*, 1134–36.

58. Seneca, *Hercules Oetaeus*, 1130–36.

The role of the cosmic conflagration and the *devotio* are intertwined, at least in Stoic thought.[59]

Emperor Otho

I must now break with the chronological pattern employed thus far. Rather than offer an examination of Lucan's Cato the Younger, as found in *Pharsalia*, I want to first briefly mention the short-reigned Emperor Otho, as it is Cato's *devotio* that will better cement our view. Otho was the second in the number of Romans to occupy the throne in 69 CE. His reign began by his assignation of Emperor Galba, the Neroian successor, and would end by his own hand.

Not much is known of Otho in regards to his personal dispositions. His biographical sketch is incomplete, with only four sources—Plutarch, Tacitus, Suetonius, and Cassius Dio—surviving. The accounts range from Plutarch's weak man to Tacitus's ruthless, cunning emperor ready to murder anyone to retain power. His manner of life is to us of no consequence except that of Suetonius's second hand information, having received something vital from his father's remembrances. According to the father of Suetonius, Otho detested civil war and never would have fought the war against Galba had he not thought it could have ended bloodlessly. This is the same reasoning behind the taking of his own life. Suetonius writes, "After the defeat, Otho at once resolved to take his own life, rather from a feeling of shame, as many have thought with good reason, and an unwillingness to persist in a struggle for imperial power at the expense of such danger to life and property."[60]

The defeat was bloody. As Plutarch recounts from first hand knowledge, even a generation after the battle, people would still remember the complete route of Otho's army and Vitellius's army slaughtering ever last Roman soldier and hoisting their bodies up for all to see. Plutarch's imagery of the scene in which Otho is told is filled with a sense of utter destruction. Though none deserted him (unlike in Suetonius's account), soldiers came to plea with him not to desert them and not to surrender! It was one soldier, however, who taking a dagger into his hand committed suicide, with his last words as "Know, O Caesar, that all of us stand in this fashion at thy

---

59. For more regarding the use of this specific language in *Hercules Oetaeus* see Lapidge, "Lucan's Imagery of Cosmic Dissolution," 310.

60. *Otho* 9.3.

side"[61] His intention was to show that the soldiers would stand to the very last behind the emperor.

It is Otho's speech, as recorded by Plutarch, that is of great importance to understanding the Emperor's death as that of ritualistic suicide:

> This day, my fellow-soldiers, I deem more blessed than that on which ye first made me emperor, since I see you so devoted to me and am judged worthy of so high honour at your hands. But do not rob me of a greater blessedness-that of dying nobly in behalf of fellow-citizens so many and so good. If I was worthy to be Roman emperor, I ought to give my life freely for my country.[62]

He concludes,

> Still, it is not to defend Italy against Hannibal, or Pyrrhus, or the Cimbri, that our war is waged, but both parties are waging war against Romans, and we sin against our country whether we conquer or are conquered. For the victor's gain is our country's loss. Believe me when I insist that I can die more honourably than I can reign. For I do not see how my victory can be of so great advantage to the Romans as my offering up my life to secure peace and concord, and to prevent Italy from beholding such a day again.[63]

What Otho gives us is an emperor, or king, who is willing to die for his people to end a crime, curse, or other evil. While Otho does not ride out like Decius Mus or seek a humiliating surrender such as is Postumius, he does offer himself as a self-sacrifice to prevent his people from suffering humiliation and defeat. What is absent in Otho's *devotio* is any sort of sacrificial dress, although the language of a religious offering is present sans the deities. As must be noted, Otho's self-sacrifice occurs during a civil war, which brings us to our final *devotio* exemplar.

Cato the Younger

The death of Cato the Younger by his own hand, a rather gruesome ending to the first Roman civil war, is a suicide, akin to that of Razias (2 Macc 14:37-46). In the historical record, the death of Cato is most likely just that, the suicide of a famous man who lost the war for the country he loved

61. Plutarch, *Plutarch's Lives* 15.3
62. Plutarch, *Plutarch's Lives* 15.4.
63. Plutarch, *Plutarch's Lives* 15.5-6.

but could not abide defeat—nor Caesar's pardon; however, this does not account for historical reinterpretation or a religious view, especially of the sort emerging so quickly after Cato's death. Long after the war had ended, the memory of the Republic had faded, the glory of the Empire had dulled, and the gods had abandoned Rome to the murderous rampages of the Caesarian line. Christianity had yet to set the world on fire. It was during this time the power of the pen was rediscovered by the poet Lucan, a young compatriot of Nero and nephew of the great orator, Seneca. His motivations are questionable, but in the end, we must contribute to his singular work the downfall and humiliation of Nero. Seeing the apocalypse approaching, Lucan chose to do battle not with sword or might, but with a shivering stylus. Whether in Roman baths or on street corners, Lucan took Nero and the whole history of Rome to task. Some years before his death (65), Lucan had started to publish the poem *Pharsalia* in which he attempted to incite a revolt by rewriting the past.[64] While Lucan reproduced the follies of Pompey, heightened the faults of Julius Caesar, and brought to light the failure of Augustus, he refashioned one person in particular as the would-be savior. By the time Lucan wrote his poem, Cato the Younger had become the epitome of the Stoic philosopher, the quintessential Roman victor, and the archetype for literary heroes.

Cato the Younger was the lesser actor in the war fought between Julius Caesar and Pompey, his place to fight for the Republic against the blatant imperial ambitions of both men. After his death, Cato had become a legend and a myth. Rather than ascending to some reward, his spirit was resurrected time and again by poets to give power to their message. Sallust, Cicero, and Virgil heralded him. Cato's fame rose until Plutarch, writing at the end of the first century of the Common Era attempted to curtail superstition and myth. It was because of Cato's sense of morality and active participation in politics that Roman stoics were able to find their synthesis. It is little wonder why Lucan chose Cato as the latent hero of his story and how Cato's divinization could be read unquestioned.[65]

Lucan must have had fertile ground from which to redraw, if such a redrawing was actually needed rather than a sharpening of the image, Cato's divinization. As C. P. Jones notes, "By the time the legend had

---

64. In a very real sense, he provided the foreword to the cataclysm that would occur during the Year of the Four Emperors by carefully drafting the destruction of the Republic, the birth of the Empire, and the abandonment of Rome by her gods only a few decades before.

65. For more on Cato's memory in Lucan, see Thorne, "Lucan's Cato."

exhausted itself, it has engendered tracts, counter tracts, biographies, and at least one play."[66] The first was Cicero's tract, followed swiftly by Julius Caesar's *Anticato*. Both are lost in whole, surviving only as fragments littering the literary landscape of the later authors. Cicero's work was an early biography rather than the rhetorical funeral eulogies that would have left open the possibility, if not the requirement, for embellishment.[67] As such, we can look at Cicero first before we move forward to other remembrances of the death of Cato.

It was not long until Cato was quite literally made into a god. Vergil the epic Latin poet, turned the suicide victim into Neptune. Victor Pöschel sees in *Aeneid* 1.148–53 the divinization of Cato via the calming of the seas.[68] Already in Vergil's lifetime (70–19), it had become allowable to proclaim Cato's name, *"quis te, magne Cato, tacitum aut te."*[69] Further, Cato, as pictured *post dictum*, is said to after his death, *"secretosque pios, his dantem iura Catonem."* While Cato's death is not recorded by Vergil, what is seen is his elevation in stature most notably because of this death.

Pliny the Elder (23–79) provides us with not only a transition to a time close to that of Jesus but gives us two important details into the development of Cato's mythology. His *Natural History*, Pliny writes, "Many other men have excelled in different kinds of virtues. Cato, however, who was the first of the Porcian family, is generally thought to have been an example of the three greatest of human endowments, for he was the most talented orator, the most talented general, and the most talented politician; all which merits, if they were not perceptible before him, still shone forth."[70] Cato is the exemplar by which others are not only measured but seemingly a rather unique paradigm. Second, Pliny is the first to give Cato the name of *Uticensis* (of Utica). As a locale attached to a name is the reward to a general after a great victory, we can only assume that Pliny, who knew of Cato's death, meant this as an honorific title. While we are left to wonder how Pliny may have viewed Cato's suicide, we can only make the reasonable suggestion that he view it as a major victory—a rather odd description if Cato's suicide was viewed only as such. What is better understood, is that Pliny was reporting—not inventing—the tradition of a major event around

---

66. Jones, "Cicero's *Cato*," 188–96.
67. Jones, "Cicero's *Cato*," 194.
68. Pöschl, *Art of Vergil*.
69. Vergil, *Aeneid* 6.841.
70. Pliny the Elder, *Natural History*, 2169–70.

Cato's death perceived as something rather like a major conquest that the crushing humiliation afforded suicide victims.

Because the *bios* of Cato's life is important to understand his death, I will now turn to Plutarch (46–120). His *Parallel Lives*, written near the end of the first century CE, details 23 lives of Grecians and Romans Plutarch believed exemplary. While not always accurate, Plutarch did from time to time call upon sources available to him. It is possible, as Jones has shown, that he used now lost sources to compose his biography of the fallen general, now a century and a half dead. While the account of Cato's death, to which we will turn to below, agrees with other historical records, it is Plutarch's record of his life that is most beneficial to our current study.

Plutarch does not shy away from giving something of a divine or sage status to Cato. In 35, Cato's wisdom and word are able to cure a king, allowing the king to see something in Cato, "Then the king, as if brought to his senses by Cato's words after a fit of madness or delirium, and recognizing the sincerity and sagacity of the speaker, determined to adopt his counsels; but he was turned back to his first purpose by his friends. However, as soon as he reached Rome and was approaching the door of a magistrate, he groaned over his own evil resolve, convinced that he had slighted, not the words of a good man, but the prophetic warning of a god."[71] In 52.2, Cato acknowledges his own prophetic prowess, "Cato therefore said: 'Nay, men, if any of you had heeded what I was ever foretelling and advising, ye would now neither be fearing a single man nor putting your hopes in a single man.' Pompey acknowledged that Cato had spoken more like a prophet, while he himself had acted too much like a friend. "

After the war was clearly lost, Cato, rather than prolonging it, decided that it was best to surrender. He was facing betrayal at the hands of his own army (61.4) and seeing that the city of Utica was likely to be destroyed, decided that rather than call his reinforcements he would surrender. However, there are several key statements made by Plutarch that allows us room to view Cato's suicide as something other than an avenue to avoid humiliation.

In 67.1, Plutarch records the last meal of the general with his cabinet as one of dialogue about the "παράδοξα καλούμενα τῶν Στωϊκῶν." In 68.2, Cato is pictured reading Plato's *Phaedo*. This is the account of the death of Socrates and the discussion of the good man who must die, but must never take his own life. Further, it is the treatise that argues for the immortality of

---

71. Plutarch, *Plutarch's Lives* 35.5.

the soul. It is during this reading Plutarch keenly forces us to observe the thought process of Cato. There, during the reading, he happens to glance up to notice his sword missing. It is not happenstance, then, that Cato is reading *On the Soul*, but it is rather a sign to us to take note of the morality of Cato's actions as compared to that merely of a suicide.

Perhaps this is why Cato, who having professed the voice of the gods, been proclaimed as a god, could state, "Now, I am my own master."[72] It is also why the people of Utica, after hearing of Cato's death would call the fallen general, fallen by his own hand, their "savior and benefactor, the only man who was free, the only undefeated."[73] Cato had committed suicide, becoming his own master and has such, the savior of the people

We now turn to Lucan's *Pharsalia*. It was written no later than 65 CE by a young poet that was once a friend of Nero. We begin in Book Nine when the author, speaking of Cato, writes, "Behold the true father of the fatherland, Rome, a man most worthy of your alters. It will never be shameful for you to swear by him, and if you will ever stand with your neck free from slavery, you will make him a god."[74] Indeed, Lucan does not consider it robbery to compare Cato with the gods or even to go so far as to draw a contrast between the virtuous Cato and the wrathful, immoral gods, "*uictrix causa deis placuit sed uicta Catoni.*"[75]

Listen while Lucan gives Cato the highest place a mortal could have,

> To thee, O Cato, pious, wise, and just,
> Their dark decrees the cautious gods shall trust;
> To thee their fore-determined will shall tell:
> Their will has been thy law, and thou hast kept it well

In the same passage, Lucan writes of Cato, "*ille deo plenus tacita quem mente gerebat effudit dignas adytis e pectore uoces.*"[76] A divine position is awarded to the man of virtue in 9.725–30. The reader must but stumble in the dark to understand Lucan is speaking of Cato as taking the place of the

72. Plutarch, *Cato the Younger* 70.1.

73. Plutarch, *Cato the Younger* 71.1.

74. Lucan, *Civil War* 9.601–4. Lucan is speaking not to the future of Cato's warrior, but to those who heard his poem. He wanted his countrymen to take up arms and to discover *libertas*.

75. Lucan, *Civil War* 1.128.

76. Lucan, *Civil War* 9.696–700, 708–10. The divine quality he carried in his mind was the (holy?) spirit of Pompey. See Lucan, *Civil War* 9.1–8

gods.[77] Why is Cato afforded this divine status? Because "Indeed, the gods withdraw from any kind of intervention in this epic, and even their existence is repeatedly questioned."[78] Cato is awarded the divine status because he acts as a god in the place of the gods.

In Book Two of *Pharsalia*. Senator Brutus visits Cato to beg him to lead the charge in favor of the Republic. The warrior acknowledges the crime of the civil war, but likewise knows that he will be made guilty by the gods. It is not mere guilt laid at Cato's feet, but something more. Elaine Fantham notes the work of two value systems in Cato's answer to Brutus. He first laughs off the suggestion he could do anything to save Rome. "Cato acknowledges . . . that he cannot by sacrificing a single life atone for all the sins of Rome and ransom her allies from the necessity of evil killing."[79]

However, after a solid pivot, Cato says,

> So be it: let the stern gods demand full atonement from Rome, nor ought we defraud war of any blood. Would that the heavenly gods and Erebus allowed this head to be doomed, to pay the penalty in full! As enemy ranks overcame Decius self-sacrificed, may both armies stab me, let barbarous hordes aim at me their Rhineland lances, may I be pierced by every spear and, standing in the middle, take the blows of the entire war. May this blood redeem whole peoples, and this sacrifice make good in kind whatever debt hangs over Romans and their ways. Why should a people submissive to the yoke, and willing to suffer brutal tyranny, perish? Drive the steel in me alone, who guards in vain our empty rights and laws.[80]

This is Lucan utilizing the religious sentimentality afforded both Cato and Decius to set the atoning expectation of Cato's death.[81] If this was an-

---

77. Likewise, the reader cannot forget the elevation of Caesar to that of a demi-god status shortly before his assignation.

78. See Bartsch, *Ideology in Cold Blood*; Lucan, *Civil War* 7.454–59. I do not mean to suggest that the same teleological abandonment is in view by both authors, although there are similar traits. Rather, I would propose Mark, his Roman audience, and any audience member who has at one time or another seen "the end of the (their) world" can relate to an sense of divine abandonment. See also the chapter specifically on Lucan in Feeney, *Gods in Epic*.

79. Fantham, *Lucan*.

80. Lucan, *Civil War* 2.320–335. See also Hengel, *Cross*, 211. He concludes his remarks on Lucan's poetic attribution of Cato's *devotio* with the words, "These words help us to understand why the earliest Christian message made sense in Rome." On Cato's plea to die in Book 2, see Seo, "Lucan's Cato," 208–11.

81. The objection here is that Lucan is writing after Paul. So is Plutarch. So is Pliny the

other time and place, we might say Lucan is theologizing Cato's death using the previous witness of Decius. He is not concerned about a physical victory, but about moral victory—comparing this victory to the fall of Decius. Cato's first worry, that his guilt and death would mean nothing, is baseless as it was his death (as he foresaw) that brought an end to the civil war.

Lucan's Cato viewed the war between Pompey and Caesar as a crime against the cosmic order, however because of his virtue he was a willing participant. At the start, he thought of nothing that could end the war, laughing at the prospect that his death could have any part in peace. The last mention of Cato reads, "Conquered Cato is rejected by the mob."[82] History gives us, however, an accepted Cato, one whose stature only rose after his death. Antiquity records well the suicide of Cato the Younger, who after an unsuccessful attempt trudged forth so that at the end of the gruesome scene, Cato lay disemboweled by his own hand at Utica.[83]

Cato's death was a reality already established in history; however, Lucan capitalized on the divine-man mythos, the man made god. From the very start of Cato's part in the poem, we are introduced to a man who knew his blood was required to stop the civil war. Further, even though his death is a historical detail, we are introduced three times to the fact Cato would die and knew so.[84] His story is one that begins with the intent that he dies for Rome, or "suicidal teleology."[85] Yet, in the end, it is not because of Caesar's sword or the snakes of Libya our hero died. Cato killed himself.

Younger. The first answer to this objection is that they inherited a recognized speculative history of Cato, beginning with Cicero and surviving by the pens of oft-unknown authors. Lucan did not invent Cato nor his popularity; rather, was able to make use of known thoughts and believes about the suicide victim to set him against Nero in the guise of the Caesar's progenitor. Further, the inherited history was one secure enough to have developed some ritualistic expectation allowing Jesus, or the early Christian communities, to adopt that same language of suicidal teleology, expatiation, and divinity as self-identification. A possible second answer would be, given the close proximity in language and thought shared between Paul and his Roman compatriots (those listed just above) is that somehow his writings were so well known as to be used by not one recognized poet, but so too two other great Roman authors. I believe the first answer is the more reasonable of the two.

82. Lucan, *Civil War* 10.53

83. Lucan never penned Utica, ending rather abruptly before Caesar's final victory. Several scholars, such as several of the Lucan scholars mentioned herein, argue that the final chapter is yet to be written or was lost. For various reasons mentioned elsewhere, I believe Lucan purposely ended his work before Cato's death and the end of the civil war.

84. Seo, "Lucan's Cato," 204n21

85. Seo, *Exemplary Traits*, 74.

This was allowed under Stoicism and as Plutarch would note, needful in Cato's case.[86] Of the five reasons given, only one pertains to us. "As a party may be broken up because of an obligation, so may life, as in the example of Menoeceus, when he sacrificed himself for his country."[87]

The *devotio* differs from other forms of voluntary death in several ways, notably because the premeditated end of the individual and of the cosmological ramifications. It is these differences made abundantly clear in the death of Cato. Let us rehearse them. The Roman General was born to die in order to save. The abandonment of Rome by the gods is ever present throughout the cases presented here. While it is latent in Decius, it becomes more pronounced in the example of Postumius. In Emperor Otho's case, like Cato, Rome was left to its own devices to wage the cosmic conflagration. To end it, or in hopes of ending it as he unlikely foresaw the rise of Vespasian, he took his own life as a sacrifice to bring peace. In Cato's case, while the myth began as a suicide, it quickly developed into an act begetting a god. What became free will was then established as that guided by Fortune, without any hint of contradiction. Vergil was the first recorded divinization of Cato, Lucan gave him the motivation of expiation, Pliny crowned him conqueror, and Plutarch savior. Especially in Cato's case, as closely identified by Lucan and Plutarch, the death had cosmological meaning. It is little wonder, then, why Cassius Dio would note that from immediately after Cato's death, he achieved the highest praise and glory.[88]

Excursus I: Cato the Younger in Early Christianity

It was not merely the Romans who admired Cato, but also early Christian writers. Tertullian, in chastising the pagans for the poor choices of their deified men, calls for the deification of Cato based on his gravity and wisdom.[89] Arnobius, writing in the third century, alludes to the deification

---

86. Zadorojnyi, "Cato's Suicide in Plutarch," 216–30. It is worth noting that Lucan's uncle has likewise committed suicide due to political reasons and he himself would soon meet that fate.

87. Sorabji, *Philosophy of the Commentators*, 357–58. See also, Sellars, *Stoicism*, 109. Sellars notes "a number of the early Stoics are also reported to have taken their own lives, including Zeno (DL 7.28) and Cleanthes (DL 7.176)."

88. Cassius Dio, *Roman History* 43.11.

89. Tertullian, *Apol.* 11.

of Cato, casting him alongside Romulus and Pompilius.[90] Notably, it was Augustine who praised Cato perhaps the loudest while condemning the Roman general for suicide.[91] In his *City of God*, Augustine presents Cato as the best Rome had to offer—one of the few who followed virtue for its sake alone.[92]

Predating Augustine is Lactantius who, while decrying suicide for the sake of suicide seems to allow Cato some pause, "All these philosophers, therefore, were homicides; and Cato himself, the chief of Roman wisdom, who, before he put himself to death, is said to have read through the treatise of Plato which he wrote on the immortality of the soul, and was led by the authority of the philosopher to the commission of this great crime; yet he, however, appears to have had some cause for death in his hatred of slavery."[93] Lactantius goes further and wonders aloud what manner of good may have come from Cato's life rather than his death. If we pause for a moment with Lactantius, he does far in remediating Cato's death towards the Christian vantage. Contrasting with Ambraciot, the Christian sees the Roman as still far superior in his self-chosen death. Why? Because Cato died for a cause, according to Lactantius. It may be this cause which allowed Jerome to see Cato as a martyr.[94]

However, one of the more important, and most unrecognized, inclusion of Cato in early Christianity may be found in the *Dialogi* of Sulpicius Severus, writing in the late fourth century. In *Dialogi* 1.3, Severus mentions Cato's march across Africa. Later, he speaks of Cato the deacon (3.10). However, in the final words to his friend (3.18), the Christian Postumianus writes what can only be an imitation not simply of Vergil, but so too Plutarch,

> But, when you have again set sail from that place with the view of making for Jerusalem, I enjoin upon you a duty connected with our grief, that, if you ever come to the shore of renowned Ptolemais, you enquire most carefully where Pomponius, that friend of ours, is buried, and that you do not refuse to visit his remains on that foreign soil. There shed many tears, as much from the working

90. Arnobius, *adv. Gent.* 3.16.

91. His reaction against Decius was opposite his censure of Cato. See Augustine, *De civ. D.* 5.18.

92. Augustine, *De civ. D.* 5.12.

93. Lactantius, "Divine Institutes," *ANF* 7:789.

94. Jerome, *adv. Jov.* 1.48.

of your own feelings, as from our tender affection; and although it is but a worthless gift, scatter the ground there with purple flowers and sweet-smelling grass. And you will say to him, but not roughly, and not harshly,—with the address of one who sympathizes, and not with the tone of one who reproaches,—that if he had only been willing to listen to you at one time, or to me constantly, and if he had invited Martin rather than that man whom I am unwilling to name, he would never have been so cruelly separated from me, or covered by a heap of unknown dust, having suffered death in the midst of the sea with the lot of a ship-wrecked pirate, and with difficulty securing burial on a far-distant shore. Let those behold this as their own work, who, in seeking to revenge him, have wished to injure me, let them behold their own glory, and being avenged, let them henceforth cease to make any attacks upon me.[95]

The allusions and echoes are profound, as Jones notes.[96] Perhaps it is worth noting that the Christian world struggled with the Roman inheritance of a defied Cato well into the Medieval Ages. Dante was known to save only two before Christ, notably our Cato and Trajan, who was saved only by the prayerful aid of a Pope.

A Jewish Model?

While this chapter points to the Roman model, there is room yet to address the possibility of a Jewish model, even if it is not usually recognized as such, notably because Jewish examples lack the rules of the Roman model as well as denying the allowance the Roman model insists it have, that of a deified man or God-man. Or, it may be that the Jewish model is all too consumed in what became Christianity, therefore any other examples in Jewish literature are unfortunately read in the light of Jesus. In this next section, I present several Jewish examples that *may* be read apart from Jesus, but help us to understand that the Roman model and Jewish model are not separated by a great gulf but may find common ground in the cultural milieu of the time.

95. Severus, "Dialogues of Sulpitius Severus," *NPNF* 11:1154.
96. Jones, "Cicero's *Cato*," 195–96.

Ananus, a Denied Devotio

If Cato died as a virtuous man to preserve the liberty of Rome, and died during a civil war, the absolute epitome of social degradation and cosmological strain, might we likewise find suitable Jewish examples to meet all, or even most, of the *devotio* requirements? If we allow for a stretching of the stipulations to include a voluntary death by riot, we may find such an example in the deaths of Ananus and Jesus, high priests during the Jewish Revolt. Both men were disposed during the siege of Jerusalem, itself a bastion of civil war as various Jewish sects fought for dominance. If, as Cato demonstrated, dying for liberty and virtue was part of the motivation for the fight, then we have something of an example of a *denied devotio*.

The speech of the now deposed high priest does not bare the semblance of deposition, but rather secures the idea that Ananus sees himself still as the role previously given to him. He notes, "Truly well had it been for me to have died ere I had seen the house of God laden with such abominations and its unapproachable and hallowed places crowded with the feet of murderers! And yet I who wear the high priest's vestments, who bear that most honoured of venerated names, am alive and clinging to life, instead of braving a death which would shed lustre on my old age. If it must be then, alone will I go and, as in utter desolation, devote this single life of mine in the cause of God."[97] As Fletcher-Louis notes, the speaker is suggesting that he is the Name, claiming for himself, even if temporarily, a divine status.[98] Later, Josephus calls the high priest "ἡγεμόνα τῆς ἰδίας σωτηρίας" who was slain in the midst of the city and as such was the beginning of the end for the Jewish revolution.

Josephus's description of the man, however, is notable. He "delighted to treat the very humblest as his equals. Unique in his love of liberty and an enthusiast for democracy, he on all occasions put the public welfare above his private interests. To maintain peace was his supreme object. He knew that the Roman power was irresistible, but, when driven to provide for a state of war."[99] The focus on liberty and democracy, mirrored in Ananus's speech (4.163–92), is similar to how Cato is said to have seen himself and definitely how his defenders saw him. Likewise, given Roman predisposition to personifying virtue especially in the person of Cato the Younger,

97. Josephus, *BJ* 4.163–64.
98. Fletcher-Louis, "Alexander the Great's Worship," 88.
99. Josephus, *BJ* 4.320.

Josephus's final account of both Ananus and Jesus is rather fortuitous. He laments, "αὐτὴν ἐπ᾽ ἐκείνοις στενάξαι τοῖς ἀνδράσι δοκῶ τὴν ἀρετήν, ὀλοφυρομένην ὅτι τοσοῦτον ἥττητο τῆς κακίας."[100]

Ananus did not take his own life, but was nevertheless slain by his fellow Jews during the midst of the chaotic siege. He was, however, afforded the sacramental vestments, a shared divinity with God, the motivation to fight for liberty, and was mourned by virtue after he died during the civil war. Further, it was his death that brought an end to the war. The only things lacking in the historiographical account of Ananus are self-sacrifice and complete divinization.

The Corporate Devotio at Masada

Like Utica, Masada is a non-battle reverberating throughout history. It is the image called to mind when one thinks of Jewish martyrdom, if not the central image, save perhaps the destruction of the Temple, of the entire Jewish Revolt. It is possible Josephus intended as such, as Masada occurred after Rome had declared victory, hosted their own triumph, and left to re-build Rome with Jewish slaves. The setting by the ancient author is meant to reflect one of cosmological considerations, albeit one that focuses squarely on the non-victorious victory accomplished by Rome.

The final battle saw the Roman commander readying his war engines to unleash all that Rome had on the remaining Jewish forces. But, "Then suddenly the wind veering, as if by divine providence, to the south and blowing with full force in the opposite direction."[101] Because of such a clear sign from above, the legions slept peacefully. During the night, however, the Jews under Eleazar to the last person took their own life. But why?

In Eleazar's speech, 7.323–36, the loss of war and the needed penalty of death is laid at the feet of those, the Sicarri, who had waged the *stasis*, or sedition, against their own *and* against Rome.[102] Their death was needed to heal the war. Further, in a later speech, Eleazar waxes Stoically regarding the death and the union with the immortal, "For it is death which gives

---

100. Josephus, *BJ* 4.325.

101. Josephus, *BJ* 7.318.

102. As will be discussed in the next chapter, divine abandonment is felt during the Roman occupation, notably because of the *stasis* Josephus attributes the destruction of the Temple to as well as the entire war. It was not mere a small act of chaos, but one that engulfed the entire world.

liberty to the soul and permits it to depart to its own pure abode, there to be free from all calamity; but so long as it is imprisoned in a mortal body and tainted with all its miseries, it is, in sober truth, dead, for association with what is mortal ill befits that which is divine."[103] He equally suggests that they take their own life to be an example to others, "We ought, indeed, blest with our home training, to afford others an example of readiness to die; if, however, we really need an assurance in this matter from alien nations, let us look at those Indians who profess the practice of philosophy."[104] Ultimately, he suggests that since God has abandoned Jerusalem and the whole of the Jewish nation due in part to their actions they must suffer the sacrifice because it is a necessity to God and will deprive Rome of what it wants, "This our laws enjoin, this our wives and children implore of us. The need for this is of God's sending, the reverse of this is the Romans' desire, and their fear is lest a single one of us should die before capture. Haste we then to leave them, instead of their hoped-for enjoyment at securing us, amazement at our death and admiration of our fortitude."[105]

This corporate suicide pact contains many of the details found in Roman literature. Only by the death of the victim will peace be achieved during the surrounding civil war. As Josephus notes throughout his work, every action during the Jewish Revolt shows that God had abandoned the Jews to the mercies of the empire. Only when the war was lost, did God finally appear and require a penalty to cease the confrontation. Mark Brighton calls this an "accent on divine authority."[106] It is not the divine abandonment at the destruction of the Temple, nor the Roman Triumph whereby all of the conquered of Judea were presented a trophy to Flavian dynasty—rather, the actual end of the war is when God returns to demand justice. This punishment is a sign of mercy and thus the end of abandonment. Only when the self-sacrifice is made does the war end and God returns to Israel[107]

CONCLUSION

As noted above, there are commonly two recognized types of Roman *devotio*, the *devotio hostium* (devotion of the enemy) and *devotio ducis* (devotion

103. Josephus, *BJ* 7.344.
104. Josephus, *BJ* 7.351.
105. Josephus, *BJ* 7.387–88.
106. Brighton, *Sicarii in Josephus's Judean War*, 142.
107. Brighton, *Sicarri in Josehus's Judean War*, 143.

of the individual). While these broad categories are generally acceptable, they must be narrowed down so as to focus specifically on the examples listed above. As such, if we take into consideration Decius and Cato, and their divinization *before* the *devotio*, what appears is a god or deified man sacrificing himself in some fashion *and* that the sacrificed is "ratified by the heavens" (per Tertullian). Further, we must understand this to include cosmological ramifications as indicated by Cato, more especially, as well as the examples of Postumius and the Jews at Masada.

As we move forward into reading Galatians, we should keep in mind our *devotio* will include the following attributes: The divinization of the devoted, either after the decision is made or recognized throughout the life of the sacrificed. This is clear in the representation of Decius and Marcus Curtius who transformed respectively into something divine after he decided to obey the priest's commands as well as Cato not only throughout Lucan's poem, but also in Plutarch's *bios* and in Cicero and Vergil's early divinization of the fallen Roman, all claiming he was something divine long before he acted, and in several authors, pointing to the reason of his action as his divinity. While Otho may not be pictured as transforming into a god, we must take into account the emperor worship naturally accompanying the Roman prince. Divinization is not merely an *aftereffect* but a *precondition* of the sacrifice. Cosmology must play an important role in this. It is not merely dying for others, but must include an attempt to achieve peace *and* to atone for crimes or sins on the national level. The "noble death," or "effective death" does not provide a sufficient answer to the cosmological aspects of the story. While sins, or crimes, are paid for via a vicarious atonement, this is not necessarily the case with either Cato or the Jews at Masada. Further, we have to investigate exactly how the sin of war, and more especially civil war, was perceived as a theological crisis by both the Romans and the Jews, not to mention the Greeks via the Athenian Thucydides.

Finally, divine abandonment must also play a part in the view of the victim, who in the place of the divine becomes divine. This final attribute ties the previous two together and is important in reading both Cato's story as well as that of the High Priest Ananus. It will become immensely important as we examine such passages as Romans 3:26 and the idea of the "διαθήκη καινή" as in Hebrews 8:13. What must not be ignored in this final aspect of our particular *devotio* is the act of reconciliation. The devoted becomes the reconciler, or the mediator, between the god(s) and the people. In the case of Lucan's Cato, he forced the gods to finally act on behalf of the

Romans to end the chaos. In the example at Masada, the death of the Sicarri was required by God's justice to reconcile Israel back to God, even if the nation remained under Roman rule.

Chapter 5

Early Christian Views on Self–Inflicted Death

INTRODUCTION

IN 2006, THE DESERT sands of ancient Coptic Gnosticism revealed a find important to our study on how Christians came to reject self-inflicted death as a viable choice. The *Gospel of Judas* (c. second century) purports to betray hidden conversations between the maligned disciple and a variation of the historical Jesus. In a scene similar to the Mount Olivet discourse in the Synoptic Gospels, Jesus and his disciples discuss otherworldly matters while using the Temple as the supreme metaphor. In this instance, Jesus rails against the priests for their sacrificing, not because of what was sacrificed (including humans) but because of the immorality of the lives of the priests.[1] This image of human sacrifice is found near the end of the weathered work as well, when Jesus tells Judas that his mission is to sacrifice the flesh of Jesus in a death that does in fact offer salvation. Rather than it railing against human sacrifice, it is better to understand the pseudonymous piece as instead supporting the use of human sacrifice, but railing against

---

1. For a discussion on the interpretation of the Temple scene, see Van Os, "Stop Sacrificing!," 367–86. Van Os argues against other interpreters that while sacrifices are to be understood as the underlying reality of the Temple metaphor, rather than seeing it as set against martyrdom, the Gnostics are using it to argue against the sacramental practices of their opponents.

the disciples—or, rather, enemies of the Gnostic author.[2] This work supplies us with the probable possibility second century Christianity viewed the death of Jesus as a human sacrifice, not unlike the sacrifices offered by other priests on other altars *and* that the sacramental practices of the Christian communities of the time reflected that insight.[3]

In the first chapter, I provided patristic readings of Galatians, from the earliest extant commentators until Augustine. In this chapter I will do the same on the topic of self-inflicted death, exactly because it was Augustine who codified the Church's understanding of self-inflicted death *against* a sect of Christians who were more than enthusiastic about martyrdom. While the history of Augustine's prohibition of the act is less malleable than some would believe, his role cannot be understated.[4] In this section, I will examine the role of self-inflicted death in various forms (usually suicide and martyrdom) developing through early Christianity from the Apostolic Fathers until Augustine.[5]

What I hope to make clear is the possibility that self-inflicted death (perhaps even an aggressive attempt at martyrdom) was not singled out for condemnation until the third century. There is a general consensus that death was to be avoided unless for the cause of Christ, but even then there is some smattering of discussion as to what counted for a death for Jesus. Why? Because the founder of the cult died a voluntary death and any straight-out condemnation must always be weighed against the death of Jesus. This points us to the very real possibility the Apostolic and Patristic authors wrestled with the method of the death (by Jesus's own will) as much they did with the effect of the death.

As will become evident, it was Augustine's reaction against the Donatists and their views of self-martyrdom that caused orthodox Christianity

2. See Jenott, *Gospel of Judas.*

3. I will assume a set of communities closely aligned set against the Gnostics and others, without assuming a strict measure or test of pre-Nicene orthodoxy. In developing the history below, I will use the sources most likely to have been recognized by successive generations, most notably by Augustine, as "orthodox."

4. See Droge and Tabor, *Noble Death,* 185. For a counter, see Amundsen, "Significance of Inaccurate History," 23. See a somewhat moderating stance on Droge and Tabor in Badham, "Final Word," 24–27. Badham argues against a complete rejection of self-inflicted death in the Early Church, at least until Augustine.

5. As with the previous chapter, I will offer a generalized examination, rather than pointedly separating examples into the three categories. Due to the face that this chapter is about the development of a codified prohibition in the face of the self-sacrifice death of the cult's leader, the focus will be on how this paradoxical development came to be.

to reconsider its views on self-inflicted death and to finally issue prohibitions against it. Until then, death by choice existed as a distant possibility, as evidenced at the very least by the continued use of martyrdom if not self-inflicted death in some of the most extreme cases of persecution—a possibility that existed exactly because the Christian cult was founded upon the voluntary death of its founder. How does one stop self-death if by the self-death of one man the world was saved?

INDIFFERENCE?

Clement of Rome, in writing to chastise a wayward congregation in a distant city, lectures the Corinthians on a variety of topics. In chapter 55, the author is writing to urge the Christians to engage in a loving self-sacrifice, to which he offers examples they are familiar with.[6]

> But moreover let us also bring forward examples of the heathen. Many kings and rulers who, being in times of pestilence, following some oracle, have given over themselves to death so that they might rescue their citizens by their own blood. Many have departed their own cities so that they might not rebel any more. We know many among us have given themselves over to imprisonment so that they might ransom others. Many have given themselves over to slavery and having received their price used the proceeds to feed others. Many women, being strengthened by the grace of God, have accomplished many manly deeds. The blessed Judith when her city was under siege, asked of the elders to permit her to go out into the fortified camp of the foreigners. Therefore, giving herself over to danger, she went out because of love for her country and for the people who were under siege, and the Lord delivered Holophernes into the hand of a woman. Not less also did Esther, perfect in faith, put herself in danger so that she might rescue the nation of Israel, which was about to be destroyed. For through fasting and her humiliation she beseeched the all-seeing Master of the ages, who upon seeing the humility of her soul rescued the people for whose sake she put herself in danger.[7]

Notable is the first verse in which Clement recounts the *devotio*. The elements (as detailed in chapter 4) are there—divine judgments, priests, and

6. For a discussion on whether or not Clement would have see these examples as historical, see Lindemann, *Die Clemensbreife*, 154.

7. Brannan, *Apostolic Fathers*.

a willing leader. In verse 2, there is the self-denial or even self-enslavement that brings about freedom for others.[8] The following verses recount Judith and Esther placing themselves in danger—likely to be killed—in order to free Israel. As Jeffers notes, "We do not know how widespread this practice was, but it tells us a great deal about the level of commitment to others that some Christians felt."[9] Such a view of Christian duty as espoused by Clement and understood by those in Corinth was likely to be ingrained in the early Christian ethos and thus may be largely dependent upon the death of Jesus as explained by a self-sacrificing death to the benefit of others. While Clement does not list self-inflicted death as a practice of the early Church, he does use it as an example of the love one is to show to another in the community, and then going past that, requires that some place themselves into slavery and danger (the likelihood of death) in order to rescue others.

The mid-second century writing, *The Shepherd of Hermas*, does address self-inflicted death. In the fourth chapter of the *Similitudes*, the angel tells the author,

> Say to all men who are able to do right, that they cease not; the exercise of good deeds is profitable to them. But I say that every man ought to be taken out from distress, for he who is destitute and suffers distress in his daily life is in great anguish and necessity. Whoever therefore rescues the soul of such a man from necessity gains great joy for himself. For he who is vexed by such distress is tortured with such anguish as he suffers who is in chains. For many bring death on themselves by reason of such calamities when they cannot bear them. Whoever therefore knows the distress of such a man, and does not rescue him, incurs great sin and becomes guilty of his blood.[10]

The context of this passage is much like the rescuing of the poor and enslaved in 1 Clement. Here, the Christian is commanded to help alleviate suffering because this drives some to suicide. Therefore, those who do not continue to do good works and thus allow suicides to take place will have that crime pinned to their account. There is no transference here, as in 1 Clement, but there is an idea that suicide for distress is not permitted, but if it happens, the crime is not necessarily to be applied to the victim.

---

8. See the discussion on Aristides use of this ancient Christian practice to defend Christianity in *Colossians and Philemon*, 242.

9. Jeffers, *Greco-Roman World*, 223.

10. Hermas, *Shepherd of Hermas* 303–5.

While 1 Clement commends the examples of self-sacrificing love and the author of *Hermes* requires Christians to work to prevent suicides brought on by distress, it is the bishop of Antioch who gives us something to consider in crossing the boundary between martyrdom and suicide. Writing at the beginning of the second century, Ignatius is found on his way to Rome, to participate in Emperor Trajan's festival. Of course, his participation seemed to be against his will and would end in his death. He is met with those of his faith who wish to do their best to rescue him from his impending death. Knowing this, he writes,

> For the beginning is well-ordered, if indeed I may obtain the grace
> to receive my lot unhindered. For I am afraid of your love, lest it
> treat me unjustly. For it is easy for you to do what you will, but it
> is difficult for me to reach God, if indeed you do not spare me.[11]

Why? Because Ignatius clearly sees that his approaching death is the best way to mimic that of Jesus. He goes so far is to say that he desires his death.[12] Rather than having his death thrust upon him, Ignatius is almost volunteering for it. To go further, he prevents his rescue and thus we must ask if this is a traditional martyrdom. He is not dying to prevent a sacrilege or blasphemy, but to mimic Jesus.

This controversy is nothing new. As Droge points out, it is possible Clement of Alexandria was commenting on Ignatius's manner of death in *Stomata* 4.17.1. Here, Clement denies that those who commit suicide (*exagein heautous*) are really martyrs.[13] Unlike Droge, however, we cannot use this example to suggest that suicide and martyrdom were "ambiguous and fluid." What is better understood is that there were some rules as to what was martyrdom and what was not-martyrdom, which could then be seen as self-inflicted death.[14] N. T. Wright is right to treat Ignatius with more care, noting that when compared to the pagans of the time, Ignatius's rhetoric is not overly suicidal.[15] Droge and Tabor, however, see Ignatius's view of this self-induced martyrdom as harkening back to Jesus's directive in Mark 8:34–35.[16] This is possibly true; however, they go too far in con-

11. Ignatius, *Romans* 1.2.

12. Given the preponderance of this theme in his epistle, it is clearly a stated treatise against rescue of the martyrs. See Ignatius, *Romans* 2.1–2; 4.1–3; 5.2–3; 6.2–3; 7;

13. See below for a discussion of Clement's views

14. Droge, "Suicide," 230.

15. Wright, *New Testament*, 364.

16. Droge and Tabor, *Noble Death*, 131.

necting the language we see by (presumably) Ignatius's own hand to other second-century examples. Christians are not dying to merely die, but they die to imitate Jesus—a situation that did cause discussion on understanding when such a necessity would actually arise.

In pointed contrast to the bishop of Antioch is the execution of Polycarp, Ignatius's Smyrnean contemporary. The tale is purported to be written several decades after the actual event, and as such, is best viewed through a refracted lens. What we can glean are but a few things. Martyrdom was still a sacred event. Polycarp was executed, could not be saved, and did not want to die. This is in direct contrast to Ignatius who begged to die. Finally, martyrs were seen as angels upon their death.[17] Further, the *Martyrdom* makes a rather bold and Stoic claim in regards to the execution—that God ordained it, "Blessed and noble, then, *are* all the martyrdoms which, according to the will of God, have taken place. For we, being more reverent, must ascribe the ruling power over all things to God."[18] Perhaps it is an argument from silence, but no less so than the argument proposed by Droge and Tabor;[19] however, the author of this work seems to indicate an execution in accordance with God's will, or perhaps at the direction of it, and one that is not. In martyrdom, unlike suicide, there is no free will.

By comparing Ignatius and Polycarp, rather than an amalgamation of suicide and martyrdom into one ambiguous concept, what we see it the recognition of death between at least two categories. Further, we see both may have been used to honor the death of Jesus. Finally, we do not see a condemnation of suicide (the latter category) per se at this stage of Christianity. It is not until Christianity speaks with a more Stoic voice do we see categories more firmly develop and as such, condemnations begin.

The Stoic Voice

The theologians of the Second Century transitioned Christianity from a provincial and Semitic religion to a cosmopolitan faith replete with schools, nuance, and history. It is not that the difference between the religion of the Jewish followers of Jesus and the faith of the Greco-Roman world is all that new, only that with a move into non-Jewish minds, the

17. See Polycarp, *Martyrdom of Polycarp* 2.3; cf. Hermas, *Similitudes* 2.2, 7; *Visions* 9.25.2.

18. Polycarp, *Martyrdom of Polycarp* 2.1.

19. Droge and Tabor, *Noble Death*, 134.

expression became something different. The exemplar of a different-but-not-new approach is Justin Martyr who, while Roman, was born in Flavia Neapolis (modern day Nablus), a city 49 km north of Jerusalem. To Christianity, he brings the introduction of Middle Platonism, a Stoic-heavy philosophy.[20] With that, he brings engrained methods of thought as well as established ethical rules. It also helped that he was trained as a Stoic philosopher.[21]

In his second apology, Justin seems to explicitly deny the use of suicide by the Christian.

> Lest any one should say to us, 'All of you, go, kill yourselves and thus go immediately to God, and save us the trouble,' I will explain why we do not do that, and why, when interrogated, we boldly acknowledge our faith. We have been taught that God did not create the world without a purpose, but that He did so for the sake of mankind; for we have stated before[22] that God is pleased with those who imitate His perfections, but is displeased with those who choose evil, either in word or in deed. If, then, we should all kill ourselves we would be the cause, as far as it is up to us, why no one would be born and be instructed in the divine doctrines, or *even* why the human race might cease to exist; if we do act thus, we ourselves will be opposing the will of God. But when we are interrogated we do not deny our faith, for we are not conscious of having done any wrong, but we do consider it ungodly always not to tell the truth, which we also realize is pleasing to God; and we also now want to free you from an unfair prejudice.[23]

He is preparing for his own trial and expected death as a Christian and is refusing the ignoble advice to simply kill himself. In the passage above he recounts what we would expect from a Stoic, even one so converted to Christ, that his life is not his own to take—that the life belongs to God. It is acceptable that others take it, as long as the Christian does not. Further, there is something others have noted—that Justin is separating the preservation of life from the duty to not take one's life.[24] For example, he did not

---

20. See Justin, 2 *Apol.* 13.2; Ferguson, *Backgrounds of Early Christianity*, 387–88.

21. See Justin, *Dialog* 2.

22 cf. Justin, 1 *Apol.* 10.

23. Justin, 1 *Apol.* 123.

24. Bernard, *Justin Martyr*, 154. See also Larson and Amundsen, *Different Death*, 103.

refrain from praising martyrs, such as Socrates.[25] What we can take from this is Justin's use of Stoicism (something he uses later in delineating the Logos) with its inherent beliefs of free will and the life as owned by God.

The unattributed second-century Letter to Diognetus contains what appears to be a statement about shunning the duty of the Christian to bear what the world gives them:

> The soul is locked up in the body, yet it holds the body together. And so Christians are held in the world as in a prison, yet it is they who hold the world together. The immortal soul dwells in a mortal tabernacle. So Christians sojourn among perishable things, but their souls are set on immortality in heaven.[26]

If we couple this with other statements (5.12; 10.7), this does not appear to be a diatribe against self-inflicted death, but about becoming more of an imitator of God. Death is evil and to be avoided, but if it is forced upon the Christian, then it will only end in their resurrection.

As noted above, Clement of Alexandria does make a distinction in the nuances of self-inflicted death. In *Stromata* 4.17.1, he takes to tasks those who call themselves Christians but commit suicide under the guise of martyrdom. While Droge may argue that the proper label is decided only by one's perspective, what is not ambiguous is Clement's continued Stoic stance against suicide.[27] He writes,

> For by going away to the Lord, for the love he bears Him, though his tabernacle be visible on earth, he does not withdraw himself from life. For that is not permitted to him. But he has withdrawn his soul from the passions. For that is granted to him. And on the other hand he lives, having put to death his lusts, and no longer makes use of the body, but allows it the use of necessaries, that he may not give cause for dissolution.[28]

Nils Pedersen, contra Droge, rather than suggesting Clement is merely prejudiced against pretenders, or somehow slighting their position, sees the whole of the Clementine corpus as a consensus of the early Christian movement that suicide is prohibited—and that aggressive martyrdom falls

---

25. See Justin, 1 *Apol.* 5.

26. Walsh, "Letter to Diognetus," 1362.

27. Droge, "Suicide," 230.

28. Clement, *Strom.* 6.9.1

under that category.[29] Pedersen does follow Origen and Tertullian as they attempt to drive a more decisive line between a death that is sacrificially self-inflicted and one that is not, revealing the struggle to differentiate between the two—a struggle shared by patristic and modern commentators alike.[30]

If there is a shadow of turning in early Christian views on the ethics and allowances of self-inflicted death, it is with the second-century schismatic and legalist Tertullian rather than the fifth-century celebrated theologian. Tertullian, a former Roman lawyer, would unlike the previous examples, not merely draw a thin line, but easily state that self-inflicted death was wrong. In *De fuga* 13.2, Tertullian sharply states the words of Jesus in the Gospels had a limit. In doing so, he ridicules the possibility of assisting someone in suicide. In his *Apologia*, Tertullian preempts Droge and Tabor's anti-Clementine argument by calling for a reasonable examination of motives.[31] I argue, however, that being the Roman he was, Tertullian likewise saw the connection between suicide and divinity, although he may not have agreed with the way the Romans believed.[32]

Tertullian is often cast as one who could not tell the difference between the various shades of self-inflicted death or had no moral direction on this issue, which is hardly typical for the Rigorist that he was.[33] Because of this, scholars and interpreters have noted his statement on Jesus's death—that it was voluntary in order to stay the executioner's tool—usually seeing it as an allowance for suicide.[34] However, as Ambrose, Augustine's mentor, would note in the fifth century, the focus of these statements (pinned to Matt 27:50), is the voluntary aspect—that it was the death of Jesus by his own will that mattered. Given Tertullian's (and others before him) state-

---

29. Pederse, "Den kristne kirkes," 241–89.

30. While we may look at intention (as sacrifice) as a dividing line, and rightly so, as we have seen the voluntary aspect is something that cannot be forgotten if we are going to properly interpret the self-inflicted death of Jesus on the grounds offered by Paul. This helps us to avoid the fallacies offered by Droge and Tabor.

31. To be fair, Droge and Tabor are not the first to make the argument for the Augustinian Reversal, but they represent the culmination of the article. For example, see O'Keeffe, "Sucide and Self–Starvation," 349–63. They seem to repeat the same non-sourced statements as found in Fedden, *Suicide*. Fedden's unsourced statements find an attempted correction in Barry, *Breaking the Thread of Life*, 52n2.

32. Tertullian, *Apol* 23.3.

33. See Gill "Response to Paul Badham," 19–23.

34. Tertullian, *Ad martyras* 4.

ments regarding the life or soul belonging only to God, the voluntary offering must be the exegetical target. This is not to say Tertullian disapproved of martyrdom.[35] He stood with Clement against aggressive (or needless) martyrdom, but also demanded that one be ready to give their life for their faith, as evident in his listing of heroic Greco-Roan suicides in *Ad Martyres*. Perhaps is what led to Tertullian's turn to Montanism. Tertullian simply draws a line between suicide and martyrdom—between giving and having life taken from you. As with others, Tertullian is simply struggling with the death of Jesus as a saving event but refraining from suggesting that a similar death is acceptable to Christians.

The Prohibition Solidification

Our two final examinees are Lactantius (c. 240–320) and Augustine. The former is often eclipsed by the latter just as the finished product often hides the differentiated pieces. In regards to Lactantius, the former imperially endorsed orator, he was quite clear that death by one's hand is to be avoided. He is clear to him there is a difference in martyrdom and suicide, and that all voluntary death is to be avoided. He writes,

> For if homicide is wicked because it is a destroyer of a man, he who kills himself is fettered by the same guilt because he kills a man. In fact, this ought to be judged a greater crime, the punishment of which belongs to God alone. For, just as we came into this life not of our own accord, so departure from this domicile of the body which was assigned to our protection must be made at the order of the same One who put us into this body, to dwell therein until He should order us to leave. And if some violence is exercised against us, it must be suffered with a calm mind, since the taking of life of an innocent man cannot be unavenged, and we have a great Judge to whom alone punishment in its entirety always belongs. They were homicides, therefore, all those philosophers and that prince of Roman wisdom himself, Cato, who before he took his life, is said to have read Plato's book on the eternity of souls. . . . But if Plato had known and had taught from whom, and how, and for whom, and for what reasons, and at what time immortality is granted, he would not have driven Theombrotus into voluntary

---

35. Except for the lavish interpretive measures, Droge and Tabor, *Noble Death*, 144–49, has a succinct accounting of Tertullian's understanding of martyrdom.

death, nor Cato either, but he would have instructed them rather unto life and justice.[36]

Lactantius does not treat well the would-be Greek martyrs and Roman heroes. He does not see them as martyrs, but as self-murderers. He stands against voluntary death just as easily as he writes towards the justification (against Donatus) of martyrs (*De Mortibus*). While he is not the first, Lactantius solidly moves the cause of Jesus' death from his hand to that of the Jews.[37] Compare this with Origen who blames the Jews, but only for failing to see that Jesus's death was offered for the benefit of all—in accordance with the Jewish Scriptures.[38]

Jacques Bels considered Augustine as the one who reversed the position of the Church on suicide.[39] As we have seen, this is not the case. Rather, I propose Augustine solidified the prohibition due to the Donatist controversy, and was able to do to so because the language of the death of Jesus had moved from a self-willed act to that of charging external culprits, namely the Jews. As with other antagonists to Augustinian orthodoxy, the Donatists soon faced defeat and in doing so, allowed the Church to be changed in ways that would last millennia.

The Donatists were a group of Christians arising after the Diocletianic Persecution, although earlier traces of their thought can be fond in the persecutions of the previous century. The Christian leaders who had obeyed Roman rule in regards to surrendering Christian artifacts and in making public allegiances of faith were considered *traditores*, having violated their Christian faith. The Donatists wanted to wipe the slate clean and replace the leaders with those who had not bowed to Rome, leading to a schism. As part of this, the Donatists held to a view of martyrdom that not only appeared to welcome death but to seek it at the hands of others. As we can see, this was not a new view nor one unsurprising give the luminaries of the faith such as Ignatius, and as this work maintains, Jesus. Augustine responded with two important works, a letter against their leader Gaudentius

---

36. Lactantius, *Divine Institutes*, 215.

37. *De. Mort. Pers. 2; Inst 4.16, 18.* Melito of Sardis, writing in the middle of the second century, was fully committed to blaming the Jews for the death of Jesus. While some modern debates attempt to blame either the Romans or the Jews, this work simply affirms without attempting to vindicate either or both parties that neither acted willingly, no more willingly than the cross itself. It was Jesus who used the actors—the Romans and the Jews—to manipulate his own death.

38. Origen, *Cont. Cels.* 2.38.

39. Bels, "La mort volontaire," 147–80.

and included a polemic in his epic, *De civitate Dei*.[40] In the latter, Augustine takes up the case of Judas, appearing to suggest that had Judas lived, he may have found forgiveness. In the former, Augustine counters the schismatic's use of 2 Maccabees 14:37–46 (see chapter 4), changing the understanding of the passage. This is not the only change Augustine wrought.

Whereas his predecessors and contemporaries had conflated the noble death with martyrdom, Augustine went further. Written near the sack of Rome, Augustine argues all self-death is a violation of the fifth commandment.[41] This includes martyrs and the Roman heroic suicides, namely Cato. Following this line of thinking, Augustine arrives at the conclusion that Cato died with dishonor, something a Christian must not do.[42] Simply, Augustine was not the first to stand against suicide in the Christian Church, but he offered narrow lines of what sort of non-natural death was acceptable, allowing him to codify Christianity's long defining stance against suicide.

CONCLUSION

We have briefly reviewed some evidences that the Christian Church's stance on the death of Jesus (and the perpetrators) changed along side that of their view of self-inflicted death. What it shows us is that the Church continued to wrestle with understanding the self-immolating Messiah alongside a developing understanding of human life. Their view, refined by sects and orthodoxy, gave way to the view somewhat universally expressed since Augustine, that any form of self-inflicted death is against the will of God. It cannot be understated how that change coincided with the change in understanding, in blaming, who caused the death of Jesus.

---

40. Augustine, *De civ. D.* 1.17–27.

41. Augustine, *De civ. D.* 1.17.

42. Augustine, *De civ. D.* 1.24–29. See also Straw, "Martyrdom," 539–40.

Chapter 6

Reading Galatians
in Light of the Devotio

INTRODUCTION

THE CONCEPT OF "PENAL substitution" in Christianity is a relatively new concept, emitting primarily from Reformation-era theologians reading the medieval theology of Anselm of Canterbury. It is not, strictly speaking, a New Testament doctrine, nor one of the early Church.[1] Given the recognition of this new fact by modern contemporary scholars and theologians, it is left to us to dig deeper into the past, even to the reality hiding beneath the interpretative emplotments of the canonical text, to discover the earliest view of the death of Jesus. It is left to us to decide, or to at least propose several reasonable suggestions as to how and why Jesus may have premeditated his own execution. Did he see it as a vicarious sacrifice, an evitable end, or was it happenstance and only an afterthought after his mission had failed?

The great challenges of New Testament scholarship of the last century seems to rest at the feet of the Historical Jesus. Scholars have spent considerable ink discovering various methods and hypotheses as to who Jesus really was, how the early Church thought of him, and perhaps even what he

---

1. It is not merely the Reformers under fire, but so too Catholic theologians—and under fire by Catholic historians. See Oxenham, *Catholic Doctrine of the Atonement*, 112–13. See also Schnell, *Theology of the New Testament*, 249–50.

thought of himself. As stated in the introductory chapter, we cannot prove the results of any actions, especially if the results are rooted in a heavenly ideal; therefore, Hermann Reimarus's challenge of the great mistake falls flat.[2] As chapter 4 proved, the quick rise of Cato Uticenius's legend, beginning almost immediately after his death, if not before, should help dispel the notions presented by Martin Kähler and Rudolf Bultmann of a stark separation between the Jesus of history and the Christ of faith.[3] It was only recently that critical scholars once again started to reunite the Jesus of history and the Christ of faith, such as N. T. Wright and Dale Allison.[4]

While the literary recounting of the death of Jesus may take many forms, we may reasonably suggest that at least one of them was somehow promoted by the historical Jesus. We can do this because of the historical examples we have of people such as Cato and Otho, among others, who planned their suicide in advance and in accordance with earlier, even religious, traditions. Thus, we can rightfully maintain that it is possible, even probable, Jesus not only knew of his impending death, but also carefully chose it and instructed his followers how to interpret it. Whether or not the results Jesus may have promised actually manifested themselves is still the unanswerable question. Because his followers not only took to the pathways to preach his message, but likewise took to the pen to scribble well the meaning of his death, we can expect to find something of the original message in the surviving works.

This final chapter is an examination of Galatians in hopes of discovering that original intent.I have provided proof that the model was known and practiced, not only in the Roman world but also in the Jewish world. I will now attempt to highlight what I believe is Paul's model in Galatians, that the death of Jesus as a self-inflicted death, and one that is self-inflicted because Jesus would have believed himself divine, embroiled in a cosmological crisis. Jesus died in such a manner because of his own self-identification, an identification Paul had come to believe was true. I will then

2. Talbert, *Reimarus Fragments*; Watson, *Gospel Writing*, 44, 62–71.

3. See Kähler, *So-Called Historical Jesus*. For Bultmann, who while believing something of the Historical Jesus existed in the New Testament nevertheless surrendered a great deal of ground of how Jesus saw himself to the abstract Christ of Faith, "I do indeed think that we can now know almost nothing concerning the life and personality of Jesus, since the early Christian sources show no interest in either, are moreover fragmentary and often legendary; and other sources about Jesus do not exist" (Bultmann, *Jesus and the Word*, 14).

4. Allison, *Historical Christ*.

attempt to meld together the various cosmological and anthropological elements while highlighting the early high Christology of Paul. All of this is done in concert with other canonical references drawn from primarily Pauline writings. Finally, I will also offer some objections along the way, but would allow these objections are Paul's attempt at rationalizing a traumatic event with which he was still wrestling. Some may call these contradictions, but simply, it is theology.

If we strip away the identification of divinity, of cosmological crisis, and of the philosophy of free will, we are left with a first-century Palestinian Jew, watching his small ethnic minority bear the boot of a cruel and oppressive regime. If we strip away the theological speculation developed even shortly after his death, what we are left with is the Jew who forced the State's police to execute him due to his possible belief that by his own death he could force the God of Israel to act. It is entirely possible the Jew in question believed himself divine, called, or chosen and acted accordingly as the plethora of examples in his world had already done. If we strip away the theology of the sacrificial death of Jesus forced upon him by God, we are left with the trauma of suicide, and it is one often repeated throughout human history. However, for now we take the trauma incurred by self-death and begin to watch as Paul builds his theology, and it is a theology I maintain is inherent in the death of this particular Jew, possibly due to the teachings of the one who, by the State's hand, killed himself.

RESTATEMENT AND REVIEW

As enumerated in chapter 4, *devotio* is the self-sacrificing meant to bring an end to a cosmic struggle. Further, the victim must be divine in some manner *before* the suicide and must complete the action of his own free will. Finally, the cosmic struggle may include some form of divine abandonment and civil war. It was not uncommon to view Israel as abandoned by God. This did not mean God was absent, but simply that because of the ongoing struggle over obedience to the covenant, God had stepped away from the Temple and from protecting his people. The covenant had been forsaken as exemplified by the sacking of the Temple in 63 BCE.[5] We may allow canonical and non-canonical authors to have their say in providing for us the cause of this disunion—simply, the sins of Israel against God.

5. See Psalm of Solomon 2, specifically verse 7. See as well, Tzoref, "Pesher Nahum," 65–84

On one hand, God demands obedience and on the other, Israel demands a reconditioning. Since both had refused to give in, both attempted to force the other side into surrender. While this may not neatly fit some definitions of "civil war," this provides a picture of two powers struggling against each other for dominance. Regardless, the war fought here is not between Rome and Israel, but between Israel and God.[6]

What was the daily outcome of this war? Rome and her brutal Emperors occupied Israel. There was a vast separation between rich and poor. There were failed messiahs, successful bandits, and a Temple veiled in Roman standards. God had been silent for hundreds of years seemingly having forgotten his covenant with Abraham, Isaac, and Jacob. There was no sign of God's promised act of rescue against the Romans.

In this desperate time, desperate measures were called for. Jesus must act. We know others attempted and failed, but if we are to believe the New Testament, Jesus was successful. In becoming the primary actor, Jesus chose the time and hour of his death. He even would go so far as to chose the type of death (Mark 8:34–38). In doing so, Jesus controlled his destiny while at the same time challenging the God who had abandoned Israel. No doubt, he truly believed he was God's son. Like Cato, he is determined and knows quite well that only he can end the war between God and Israel.

Therefore, the death of Jesus cannot be laid at the feet of God and his blood is not upon the hands of either the Jews or the Romans. Rather, Jesus offered himself up as a ritual *devotio*—that is, like Cato and others before him, Jesus committed suicide in order to force an end to God's abandonment of Israel, exercising the momentous act of free will that only a divinity could.[7] Neither the Jews nor the Romans are instruments of God in the sacrifice of Jesus, because God simply has no active role in the death of Jesus—they are the instruments of Jesus. We are allowed this suggestion in the passiveness of Paul's language, the notion that Jesus became sin to remove our trespasses, and died as breaking the Law (Gal 3:13). That he allowed himself to be killed is also remembered in later Gospels (John 10:18).

6. This reading is supported by Eph 2:13–17.

7. For other scholars, even slightly, connecting the death of Jesus to *devotio*, see Kiley, "Roman Legends," 135–42; Doran, "Narratives of Noble Death," 385–99; Collins, "Finding Meaning," 175–96.

READING THE DEATH OF JESUS AS DEVOTIO

In the following section, I will attempt to bring in certain elements I believe help secure the overall thesis of this work. I will follow a recent scholar who posits *Christ* as the honorific, which I count along that of Cato's. I will examine Paul's *propositio*, divine sonship, divine abandonment, and finally, a reading of Galatians 3:13. I hope that the brevity of this chapter is made up by the examples of both Jewish and Roman suicidal deaths, allowing the argument to be made that Paul used a model the Romans and the Jews would have known, and understood the implications thereof, if not having received the model from pre-Pauline sources, added the theological speculation we now know as Galatians.

How Jesus *Became* Χριστὸς

In his recent work, Matthew V. Novenson concludes Χριστὸς is an honorific, following the normal Greco-Roman strategies.[8] He cites a list of Greco-Roman examples as well as one related to the Judaism of the day (1 Macc 6). In fact, we can look at the honorifics assigned to the topics of a range of books—the Maccabees. As he also notes, a later would-be Messiah, Shimon bar Kosiba, was robed of his surname by history and had it replaced with Kokhba, a honorific meaning "son of the star." At the time of Paul's writing, honorifics played a role in transporting stories of victories and other heroic feats. Further, he also notes, "Grammarians of the imperial period also include under the heading 'agnomina' the *cognomina ex virtute*, or victory titles, that is, honorifics corresponding to the place names of successful campaigns by military leaders."[9] Unlike Augustus or the Hasmoneans, Jesus' honorific does not come by a military victory. Rather, more akin to Cato Uticensis, it is the very manner of the death of Jesus that gives him an honorific.

While Novenson and others see no difference in whether or not Paul places Χριστὸς before or after the given name, it may not always be the case, especially in Paul's earlier writings as he is thinking through his understanding of who Jesus is. It may be important and helpful in our overall argument to examine the several times in Galatians Paul uses the honorific first (Gal 2:4; 3:14, 26–28; 4:14; 5:6, 24). While the placement of the

8. Novenson, *Christ Among the Messiahs*, 87–97.

9. Novenson, *Christ Among the Messiahs*, 79.

honorific may indicate an intention by Paul, it is not necessary to secure our present argument, as it is the honorific itself that aids the argument.

In Galatians 2:4, we find war-like language suggesting some false believers are infiltrating in order to discover the ἐλευθερία of the Galatian church. As Martyn notes, "When Paul's messenger had completed the reading of the letter, the Galatians will have sensed that, in writing to them, Paul had chosen to place great weight on the noun 'freedom.'"[10] He goes on to write, "Especially important is the fact that Paul does not speak of freedom as an abstraction, as an ideal, or as a state of mind that can be achieved, let us say, by learning to view all things external to the real self as matters of no consequence (the Stoic *ta adiaphora*)."[11] Given the view of "freedom" found in Greco-Roman thought, and the way Paul uses it, perhaps this is Paul's way of highlighting the honorific, but associating it directly with the outcome of the cosmic battle. We may also see this in 3:26–8 as Paul positions Jesus as the one who unites all (or makes) free persons through his death. In 5:6 and 5:24, Paul is speaking to those won by Christ through his death. If, as we discussed in chapter 2, Paul is contrasting the arena with life in Christ, then 5:24 takes on a different light.

It may be that Paul's mixing of the name and title has little to do with intent, but is more of a style choice. While I can easily suggest placing the honorific before the name means something in the above-mentioned passages, I find it difficult to suggest with any validity the same for 2:16 and 4:14. I will now turn to examining Galatians 2:20–21 and, more importantly, Galatians 3:1–14.

Paul's Propositio: *Galatians 2:20–21*

As de Boer points out, the last few verses of the chapter is "the theological high point of the first two chapters and crucial to the interpretation of the remainder of the letter."[12] As discussed in chapter 1, Galatians 2:20–21 has played a role in Christian interpretation, notably by Victorinus who read in the passage the victorious Christ, liberator of all. Other Christian commentators, such as Jerome, would wrestle with the free will offering of Jesus. Jerome twisted his commentary, ranging from acknowledging what Paul said, allowing that it was God who handed over Jesus, that Jesus did so

10. Martyn, *Galatians*, 196.

11. Martyn, *Galatians*, 219.

12. De Boer, *Galatians*, 159.

to honor the Father's will, and finally laying blame on Judas and the leaders of the Jewish people.[13] Notwithstanding the difficulties in this passage, it is worth noting Paul's foreshadowing here, that it is Jesus who decided to die for all.

It may be necessary to read this passage with Galatians 1:4, and in doing so, seek to understand just how active Jesus is in his death. F. F. Bruce calls Galatians 1:3-4 "probably the earliest written statement in the NT about the significance of the death of Christ,"[14] and it is repeated—the self-sacrificing statement—throughout Galatians and explained thoroughly in 3:1-14. Betz suggested these statements "implies an old christology which understood Jesus' death as an expiatory self-sacrifice."[15] This Christological tie to the language of voluntary death continues in 2:20 and in 3:13.[16]

However, there is the matter of whether or not 1:3-4 (and 4:4) points us to Jesus as a passive actor, and thus disrupting this current thesis. Was Jesus a mere actor on a stage, or was he his own first principle in his death? Hooker suggests Paul reads Jesus here as the actor, rather than the script performer. "When Paul explores the theme of redemption . . . and the way in which God has dealt with the plight of mankind . . . Jesus' own role is understood as less passive and more active: he is not only 'given up' by God on our behalf (Rom 8:32) but 'gives himself up' for our sakes."[17] Following part of Longenecker's suggestion, I propose we read κατὰ τὸ θέλημα τοῦ θεοῦ καὶ πατρὸς ἡμῶν as appending to those who are rescued, something within Paul's theological realm (as well as that found in Luke 2:14).[18] As Witherington notes, "The Mosaic Law and obedience to it is not, in Paul's view, how one got into Christ, how one stays in Christ, or how one goes on in Christ. It is no longer what defines and delimits who the people of God

---

13. Jerome, *Galatians* 1.2.20.

14. Bruce, *Galatians*, 77.

15. Betz, *Galatians*, 41.

16. de Boer, *Galatians*, 162.

17. Hooker, "Interchange and Atonement," 480.

18. Longenecker, *Galatians*, 9. While I propose to follow part of this suggestion, it is not completely out of the realm of thesis so see all of this unfolding according to some heavenly plan. What is known is the voluntary death of Jesus, something Paul attests and scholars support so that it may be the "will" is more along the lines of what is acceptable to God rather than God's directing of it. That is for the theologians to decide. The same may be said for Galatians 4:4, as well as the Fates and Fortune controlled Cato's free will suicide.

are and how they ought to live and behave."[19] It is a valid assumption, then, to append Paul's appeal to the will of God to the rescue performed by Christ (as opposed to the rescue by the Law). It is worth noting John Chrysostom (fifth century) used this passage to combat his opponents who appeared to follow the Donatist suicides.[20]

Turning to 2:20-21, we see the same active death as the foundation for Paul's worldview; however, as both Betz and Longenecker agree, "τοῦ ἀγαπήσαντός με καὶ παραδόντος ἑαυτὸν ὑπὲρ ἐμοῦ" are Christological adjectives.[21] As we will see, Paul's understanding of a divine Jesus is not something fostered upon him by a later Nicene speculation, but one inherent in the Apostle's view of the Messiah who "gave himself up." Further, Paul's "life" in 2:19 and the contrast with Sirach 17:11 and 45:5 maybe explain the "curse" in 3:13, all through the lens of Jesus choosing death.[22]

Galatians 2:20-21 is a ground fertile for theological speculation. However, what we should focus on for this work is the Christology continued therein—that it is connected to Jesus' self-love and self-death. Paul is not writing unintentionally, rather, he is composing a carefully articulated statement preparing his readers for what is to come. He gives us what we need, first in 1:3-4 and now in 2:20-21 so that we have heard twice his concern about how to view the death of Jesus and what benefits it has wrought. With the *propositio* firmly planted, Paul moves now to explain to us the crucifixion.

Pauline Sonship

As clear in Galatians 1:3-4 and 2:20-21, the epistle is about the death of Christ and the benefits afforded to those rescued. As we have seen in Galatians 2:20, Paul connects the death of Jesus to his status as Son of God, indicating a divinity inherent in the crucified Jew. This is not meant to say Jesus was deified because of his death, but to enforce the thesis Jesus died because of his deity. That Paul saw Jesus as deity before his death is best realized in the Christological Hymn in Philippians 2.

---

19. Witherington, *Grace in Galatia*, 172.

20. See his Homilies on Galatians at this verse.

21. Longenecker, *Galatians*, 94.

22. See the discussion in Garlington, *Galatians*, 166–67, for Paul's use of death as life as an ironic contrast with previous commentators' view on the Law as life.

Philippians 2:5–11 has a storied history among recent scholarship. As scholars often point out, not only are there different interpretations, but reviews are mixed as to whether or not this was of Pauline origin.[23] Ernst Käsemann points to a gnostic background.[24] It is possible, but doubtful Paul needed to visit the Gnostics to learn about the divinity of Jesus. The notion of a person holding divinity and dying as part of that divinity surrounded Paul. The etiology of the descent portion of the hymn, which is where Käsemann aligns with Gnostic influence, can be seen in 1 Thessalonians as well as Galatians 4:4. Eduard Schweizer suggested the hymnic figure is *the righteous sufferer*.[25] He draws much of the evidence of his conclusions from 2 Maccabees 7 and Isaiah 53. Later, he would incorporate the Jewish Wisdom tradition, coming close to Dieter Georgi.[26] Georgi suggested the hymn finds its origins in the Wisdom of Solomon.[27]

At this point, I want to turn to interpretations of the hymn offered by Paula Frederickson and Larry Hurtado, interpretations I believe that aids the alignment of the background with the *devotio* model as well as the nuanced suggesting that the divine language found in the hymn may originate with Jesus. As she notes, the Greek of Paul's letter does not include two deities, but suggests Jesus was divine "'in the form of [*a*] god.'" Due to Jesus forsaking whatever that may mean and instead sacrificing himself especially on the cross, the Most High God rewarded him with an elevated status.[28]

Hurtado cautions readers against "metaphysical speculation" around what the deity or divinity of Jesus may mean, rather focusing on the "self-humbling" Jesus endures in 2:6–8.[29] For our purposes it is the "metaphysical speculation" we must consider, especially given the very nature of the *devotio* is one demanding a sacrifice of divinity. I am in agreement with Hurtado who, after much discussion, concludes this passage "refer(s) to Jesus as being in some way 'divine' in status or mode, and then becoming a

---

23. See Reumann, *Philippians*, 333–35, for some of the discussions involving various issues with this passage.

24. Käsemann, "Critical Analysis," 45–88.

25. Schweizer, *Erniedrigung*, 35–44, 51–54

26. Schweizer, *Erniedrigung*, 5, 99

27. Georgi, *Zeit*, 263–93

28. Frederickson, *Pagan's Apostle*, 137–39.

29. Hurtado, *How on Earth*, 97.

human being."[30] Further, he writes, "In these verses Jesus is the sole actor, and his deeds tend entirely in the direction of self-abnegation, service, and obedience, even to the point of a cruel death."[31] To go further, Hurtado sees in the pericope the possibility that such language goes back to the earliest Christian community. He states, "The tradition of the earthly Jesus was influential in shaping both this description of his actions, and possibly early Christian paraenesis." He feels safe writing that the pre-existence as described by Paul is "described after the fashion of the observed, historical action."[32] He is not alone.

This is only meant to be a very brief statement on Paul's understanding of Jesus as divine. Represented here are two points on the spectrum, both agreeing Paul saw Jesus as divine (in some way).[33] Further, it is possible this "hymn" predates Paul and the Pauline communities. Thurston may posit this hymn as one deriving from earlier ones, even as early as the 40s.[34] If Hengel is correct, that the earliest hymns to Jesus were derived from the Messianic readings of particular Psalms, then again we can trace the development of a high Christology to an early, pre-Pauline, time—if not certainly to Jesus, then we can trace this pre-Paul high Christology to the Apostles.[35] The *raison d'être* is the *devotio* that would require a divine Jesus, a divine Jesus who was specific in his teachings and death.

Abandonment?

As addressed in chapters 4 the idea of divine abandonment (or absence) is a necessary one in understanding not only need for a *devotio* but also the possible motivations of Jesus acting by his own free will and hand to

30. Hurtado, *How on Earth,* 101.

31. Hurtado, *How on Earth,* 104.

32. Hurtado, "Jesus as Lordly Example," 113–126. Hurtado is insistent, and rightly so, that the earliest devotion to Jesus is not borrowed from Greek Pagan cults, but can be found amount both Aramaic and Greek speak followers, thus finding a genesis of language in the LXX or other Hebrew Scriptures. See Hurtado, *Lord Jesus,* 20–21. Somewhat following Martyn, Hurtado also sees in John actual language used to expel Jewish-Christians from the synagogue. See Hurtado, *Lord Jesus,* 402n107; cf. Hurtado, *How on Earth,* 101.

33. For a larger and more lengthy treatment of recent views on this passage, see Reumann, *Philippians,* 334–38

34. Thurston, *Philippians and Philemon,* 77–78.

35. Hengel, *Studies,* 116.

commit the act. While we know that the idea of divine abandonment did survive in Paul's cognitive environment, I believe we find evidenced that it was something he included in Galatians to help solidify his overarching argument. This is found rather clearly in Galatians 4:21–27 as Paul uses the then-current situation in Jerusalem, that of one "desolate"—that of one abandoned by God.[36] Paul is contrasting not jut the earthly and the heavenly, but the one abandoned by God and the one liberated by Jesus.[37] We may also consider the discussion of the Gentiles, previously abandoned by God, in Galatians 3 as part of this trope. In fact, chapter 3 and 4 may be better read as that of Israel and the Gentiles in Exile.[38] Further, Paul's use of "curse" may be tied to Deuteronomy 27–32, wherein Israel is faced with, having not obeyed the Book of the Law, an exile, or divine abandonment —and God is prevented from or unwilling to accept repentance and had certainly always been set against the Gentiles. James Scott connects this possible reality to the language used in Galatians 3:10.[39] This may have been a common thought among Paul's fellow Jews.[40] If this is the case, then the end of exile—of both the Jews and the Gentiles—is seen in Galatians 3:1–14: Jesus' death ends the curse, the abandonment by God, for both peoples.

Is Paul lamenting exile or something else? In rereading Galatians 3:1–14 through the lens of *devotio*, do we not discover something deeper than the usual assumption "Jesus died for our sins?" Can we better understand Paul's anger? If we return to Rabbi Ishmael's understanding of Jonah and the honor of God, we find Paul issuing charges against not the Gentiles or the Jews, necessarily, but the one who first gave the law, or rather, in Paul's words, the "curse of the law." The Law stands counter to faith (Gal 3:7–8). It is the Law that first divided the Jew and the Gentile as well as the Law that led to the curse (divine abandonment). We find the promise of divine abandonment in Deuteronomy 32:15–20, so that if Israel fails to live up to the Law, God will abandon them.[41] Further, as Isaiah 43:28 and 44:1–5

---

36. Silva, "Galatians," 809. This is not to say Paul believed the Jewish people abandoned (cf. Rom 9–11).

37. Lopez, *Reimagining Paul's Mission*, 154.

38. Hafemann, "Paul and the Exile," 329–72.

39. Scott, "Works of the Law," 187–221.

40. Silva, "Galatians," 800. For a discussion on this point, see Das, *Paul*, 153–55; *Paul and Jews*, 38.

41. Patterson and Hill, *Hosea–Malachi*, 184.

suggests, this "curse" by God will lead to a creation of a new people.[42] Paul's anger, then, may be directed against those who prefer divine abandonment as caused by the "curse of the law" to the creation of a new people, especially if those new people are charging themselves with defending God's honor. It is also possible Paul is walking a very tight line in the way he speaks about the God who gave the law.

The Curse in Galatians 3:13

What is the curse? We often find scholars pointing to the cross as a curse, with the almost automatic suggestion that a crucified Messiah would have caused no little disconcertion among Jesus' (and Paul's) fellow Jews. As Fredrikson notes, this notion should be put to rest, although I believe she misses the mark as to why the message of Paul was so offensive.[43] 11 Q Temple does suggest Paul's interpretation of Deuteronomy 21:23 is accurate at least for some sectarians; however, no document of the time actually suggests the curse is the act of the cross. Fredrickson provides several examples of the time wherein bodies were displayed by hanging (the original intent of the passage in Hebrew) and Jews were crucified, without the appendage of the person "being cursed." She then goes on to connect the curse in this passage to the blessing and curse cycle of Deuteronomy, but this is in my opinion, unconvincing, and the more so when we consider the proposed manner in which Jesus died, that of *devotio*—or, more bluntly, suicide.

Betz wonders aloud, "γενόμενος ὑπὲρ ἡμῶν κατάρα . . . this statement presupposes sacrificial ideas which are, however, not spelled out. Does Paul mean that Christ became the *object* of the curse in place of us, or a 'curse offering' as a means of propitiation 'for us'? Is the notion derived from Judaism, from the pre-Pauline tradition in Gal 4:4–5 or is it a formulation *ad hoc*? A definitive answer cannot be given."[44] Counter Betz and Lohse, there is a definitive answer.[45] As with the discussion on the "hymn" in Philippians 2, "the statement is based upon a pre-Pauline interpretation of Jesus' death

---

42. Goldingay and Payne, *Isaiah 40–55*, 316–18.

43. Fredrickson, *Pagan's Apostle*, 83–84.

44. Betz, *Galatians*, 150–51. See also Dahl's remarks where he, too, sees Gal 3:13–14 as "a fragment of a pre-Pauline tradition" (Dahl, "Atonement," 153–54).

45. Lohse proposed the *ad hoc* interpretation. See Lohse, *Märtyrer und Gottesknecht*, 155.

as a self-sacrifice and atonement."[46] If Paul had in mind here the *devotio*, then this is the answer Betz and many others have sought—and it is the answer that does not require a lot of stretching to accommodate. We can add Job 2:9 to our discussion about Jewish suicide in chapter 3 as well as rehearse the death of Judas who by his (atoning?) suicide cursed his land. What is the answer? As in Paul's *prospostio*, the "curse" is the divine Jesus offering himself up for the sake of Israel and now the Gentiles to fulfill the Law, which meets the presentation offered by early Christian commentators in chapter 1, and hopefully, throughout this work.

I will suggest one other possible meaning shrouded in this verse, following the theme of divine abandonment. If there was a tradition of Jesus issuing some cry from the cross (cf. Mark 15:34) or of some tradition of Jesus seeing himself as a *devotio*, then we might read Paul's reception of that tradition here in Galatians 3:13. It then becomes possible Jesus counted himself as the representative of Israel abandoned by God, and as such, was truly "cursed" according to Deuteronomy 21:23. "The body of a malefactor hanging on a tree represented divine abandonment. This Christ became."[47] Jesus becomes the abandoned in order to force God to act and in doing so is rewarded.[48]

SUMMARY AND FORWARD

People completed the *devotio*—an act of suicide with the intention that such a death could change the cosmos—in times of great anguish, when they or their charge (a city, an army, a nation) were slated by the gods to be vanquished. They did so by their own free will, and if not by their own hand, then premeditated it so that others would be forced to do it for them. It does not rob them of their own control, but instead forces us to consider how much thought they placed upon their own death. In several cases presented above, the self-victim was seen as divine, which allowed them a measure of free will not granted to ordinary mortals. And in each time it appears they were successful. Decius won his war, Otho his short-lived Pax Romana, Cato his honorific, and Jesus the liberation of the cosmos—the inclusion of the Gentiles into covenant with the God of the Jews.

46. Betz, *Galatians*, 151.

47. O'Conor, *Galatians*, 53.

48. von Balthasar, *Creator Spirit*, 201.

I maintain Paul's use of this particular model is one that pre-dates him, and possibly can be traced to the one who had himself murdered on a cross. We see scholars acknowledge Paul's statements on the death of Jesus predate him and struggle with the verses in question as to what they may actually mean. By placing Jesus alongside other self-actors, I hope to have settled some of these questions as well as turned the guilt of the death of Jesus away from the Jews, the Romans, or even us, and placed it where it originally was—at the feet of Jesus. I do not believe this model is ever distant from other New Testament authors, and is certainly reused in Paul's writings. Further, we know by early accounts that self-sacrifice was sometimes part of the Christian life. Simply, the early Church celebrated the death of Jesus as one of a suicide by a divine son because they believed it had accomplished exactly what it was meant to.

As Dauzat has noticed, the death of Jesus in the Gospel of John is self-inflicted (see chapter 1). Perhaps John is giving us a clue in 8:22. We find this in the Synoptics as well, particularly in the pronouncements in Mark 8:31–33; 9:31–32; 10:32–44. These announcements might hold a tradition, particularly in Mark 8:31–33 of the disciples reacting to the coming self-inflicted death of their teacher. Compare this to Matthew 16:21–23 and the reaction from Peter becomes more pronounced. In the later passage, Jesus is clearly connecting his coming death, one he is forcing, to his divinity. Mark 10:45 is a clear statement that Jesus held a "suicidal teleology" (see above). As discussed above, the words of Jesus on the cross, making use of Psalm 22, may also indicate a theme of self-inflicted death is present, not to mention the entire scene in the garden. The author of Hebrews notes something akin to the "hymn" in Philippians, connecting the humbling of a divinity and the need for the divinity in order to become a sacrifice (Heb 2:17–14; cf. Heb 10:12–14). Ephesians 5:2; Titus 2:14; 1 Peter 2:24 also shows a concept of a self-sacrifice of Jesus. And again, we circle back to the very words of Paul, or rather the words he may have inherited, of a man who was the primary actor in that which led to his death. I am hopeful the present thesis will find more support in the New Testament canon in future works.

Chapter 7

Conclusion

I HAVE ATTEMPTED TO write this work with a somber, conservative tone with the reception of this work always in mind. It is difficult for many to read the word suicide and while I understand that, I find it necessary to continue to understand the death of Jesus as a premeditated, self-inflicted death that, if we strip away the theology and self-motivations, is nothing less than a suicide. Jesus, according to the Gospels, came to die and was intent on accomplishing this mission. Paul picked the language up of a suicide victim who believed he was divine and because he was divine, must offer himself freely as human sacrifice. This was not Paul's creation, but as I have maintained, not only pre-dates him, but may likely be derived from Jesus.

The hope of this model is that it not only alleviates the application of external guilt (the Jews/Romans killed Jesus/Jesus died for my individual sins) as well as the charge of "child abuse" so often leveled at the Father of Jesus, but it may help to understand the mechanism of the atonement. The devotio, then, is the method whereby the atonement is allowed to work. The self-sacrifice of the divine Son of God, made in love, brings peace by not merely restoring the covenant, but renewing it by expansion. Unlike Jonah who would have died to preserve God's honor to prevent him from saving Nineveh, Jesus is dying to preserve God's honor to the Deuteronom-ic covenant, allowing him to keep his promises while being reconciled to not just Israel, but the entire cosmos. While I do not believe one work can change Christian theology, it is my wish Christians better understand their language of guilt as applied to who was actually the charged party in the cosmic court held at the Crucifixion. Perhaps this is why, standing solitary in the Garden of Gethsemane, Jesus addressed a God who was not listen-ing, praying, "Let this cup pass from me…" only to later substitute himself for Israel and all of the cosmos, crying, "My God, my God… why have you abandoned me?"

A Bibliography of Selected Works

Aitken, Ellen B. *Jesus' Death in Early Christian Memory: The Poetics of the Passion*. Göttingen/Fribourg: Vandenhoeck & Ruprecht, 2004.

Ambrosiaster. *Commentaries on Galatians—Philemon*. Translated by Gerald L. Bray. Downers Grove, IL: IVP Academic, 2009.

Angelo, Brelich. *Religioni E Civilta*. Vol. 1. Rome: Edizioni Dedalo, 1972.

Asso, Paolo. *Brill's Companion to Lucan*. Leiden/Boston: Brill, 2011.

Attridge, Harold W. *Hebrews: A Commentary on the Epistle to the Hebrews*. Philadelphia: Fortress, 1989.

Avemarie, Friedrich, and Jan Willem van Henten. *Martyrdom and Noble Death: Selected Texts from Graeco-Roman, Jewish, and Christian Antiquity*. London/New York: Routledge, 2002.

Barry, Robert L. *Breaking the Thread of Life: On Rational Suicide*. New Brunswick, NJ: Transaction, 1996.

Bates, William N. "Archaeological Discussions." *American Journal of Archaeology* 14.4. (1910) 485–540.

Battin, Margaret Pabst. *Ethical Issues in Suicide*. 2nd ed. Englewood Cliffs, NJ: Pearson, 1994.

Bauernfeind, Otto. "Τρέχω, Δρόμος, Πρόδρομος." In *Theological Dictionary of the New Testament*, edited by Gerhard Kittel, et al., 226–35. Vol. 8.Grand Rapids, MI: Eerdmans, 1964.

Baumgarten, Joseph M. *Studies in Qumran Law*. Leiden: Brill, 1977.

Beacham, Richard C. *Spectacle Entertainments of Early Imperial Rome*. New Haven: Yale University Press, 1999.

Beal, Timothy, and Claudia V. Camp. *The Fate of King David: The Past and Present of a Biblical Icon*. Edited by Tod Linafelt. Reprint, New York: T. & T. Clark, 2012.

Beard, Mary. *A History*. Vol. 1 of *Religions of Rome*. Rev. ed. Cambridge/New York: Cambridge University Press, 1998.

Bechtel, Daniel Rodney. *The Exegesis of Galatians 2:14–21 by the Early Greek Fathers and the Major Recent Commentators*. Madison, NJ: Drew University Microfilms, 1986.

Berg, Inhee C. *Irony in the Matthean Passion Narrative*. Philadelphia: Fortress, 2014.

Betz, Hans Dieter. *Galatians*. Philadelphia: Fortress, 1989.

Bird, Michael F., and Joseph R. Dodson. *Paul and the Second Century*. London/New York: T. & T. Clark, 2011.

Blidstein, Gerald J. *Honor Thy Father And Mother: Filial Responsibility in Jewish Law And Ethics: Augmented Edition*. Jersey City, NJ: KTAV, 2006.

A Bibliography of Selected Works

Bloch, Sidney, and Stephen Green, eds. *Psychiatric Ethics*. 4th ed. Oxford/New York: Oxford University Press, 2009.

Boin, Douglas Ryan. *Coming Out Christian in the Roman World: How the Followers of Jesus Made a Place in Caesar's Empire*. New York: Bloomsbury, 2015.

Boisseier, Melanges. *Receuil de mémoires concernant la littérature et les antiquités romaines: Dédié à Gaston Boissier à l'occasion de son 80e anniversaire*. Paris: A. Fontemoing, 1903.

Bouchier, Edmund S. *Sardinia in Ancient Times*. London: Forgotten Books, 2012.

Breytenbach, Cilliers. *Grace, Reconciliation, Concord: The Death of Christ in Greco-Roman Metaphors*. Leiden/Boston: Brill, 2010.

Brighton, Mark Andrew. *The Sicarii in Josephus's Judean War: Rhetorical Analysis and Historical Observations*. Atlanta, GA: SBL, 2009.

Bultmann, Rudolf. *The History of the Synoptic Tradition*. Oxford: Blackwell, 1963.

Cain, Andrew, and Josef Lössl. *Jerome of Stridon*. Edited by Andrew J. Cain and Josef Lossl. Farnham, UK/Burlington, VT: Ashgate, 2009.

Cain, Andrew, and Noel Lenski. *The Power of Religion in Late Antiquity*. Farnham, UK/Burlington, VT: Ashgate, 2010.

Carcopino, Jérôme. *Aspects mystiques de la Rome païenne*. Paris: L'artisan du livre, 1942.

Cholbi, Michael. "Suicide." In *The Stanford Encyclopedia of Philosophy*. Edited by Edward N. Zalta. 2013. https://plato.stanford.edu/archives/fall2017/entries/suicide.

Ciampa, Roy E. *The Presence and Function of Scripture in Galatians 1 and 2*. Tübingen: Coronet, 1998.

Clark, Mary T. "A Neoplatonic Commentary on Christian Trinity: Marius Victorinus." *Neoplatonism and Christian Thought*, edited by Dominic O' Meara, 24–33. New York: SUNY, 1982.

———. "The Neoplatonism of Marius Victorinus the Christian." In *Neoplatonism and Early Christian Thought: Essays in Honour of A.H. Armstrong*, edited by A. H. Armstrong, et al., 153–59. London: Variorum, 1981.

———. "The Psychology of Marius Victorinus." Edited by Allan D. Fitzgerald, O.S.A. *Augustinian Studies* 5 (1974) 149–66.

Cohen, Jeremy. *Sanctifying the Name of God: Jewish Martyrs and Jewish Memories of the First Crusade*. Philadelphia: University of Pennsylvania Press, 2006.

Collins, Adela Yarbro. *Mark: A Commentary*. Edited by Harold W. Attridge. 2nd ed. Minneapolis: Fortress, 2007.

Collins, Adela Yarbro, and John J. Collins. *King and Messiah as Son of God: Divine, Human, and Angelic Messianic Figures in Biblical and Related Literature*. Grand Rapids, MI: Eerdmans, 2008.

Cooper, Stephen A. *Marius Victorinus's Commentary on Galatians*. Oxford/New York: Oxford University Press, 2005.

Cooper, Stephen A., and David G. Hunter. "Ambrosiaster Redactor Sui: The Commentaries on the Pauline Epistles (Excluding Romans)." *Revue d'Etudes Augustiniennes et Patristiques* 56.1 (2010) 69–91.

Crossan, John Dominic. *The Cross That Spoke: The Origins of the Passion Narrative*. Eugene, OR: Wipf & Stock, 2008.

Dabourne, Wendy. *Purpose and Cause in Pauline Exegesis: Romans 1.16–4.25 and a New Approach to the Letters*. Cambridge/New York: Cambridge University Press, 1999.

Dauzat, Pierre-Emmanuel. *Le suicide du Christ: Une théologie*. Paris: Presses universitaires de France, 1998.

DeMaris, Richard E. *The New Testament in Its Ritual World*. London/New York: Routledge, 2008.

Di Berardino, Angelo. "Suicide." In *Encyclopedia of Ancient Christianity*, edited by Angelo Di Berardino and James Hoover, 650–52. Translated by Joseph T. Papa, et al. Downers Grove, IL: IVP Academic, 2014.

Dodds, E. R. *Pagan and Christian in an Age of Anxiety: Some Aspects of Religious Experience from Marcus Aurelius to Constantine*. Reprint. Cambridge/New York: Cambridge University Press, 1991.

Donnelly, John, ed. *Suicide: Right or Wrong?* 2nd ed. Amherst, NY: Prometheus, 1998.

Dozeman, Thomas B. *Exodus*. Grand Rapids, MI: Eerdmans, 2009.

Droge, Arthur J. "Mori Lucrum: Paul and Ancient Theories of Suicide." *Novum Testamentum* 30.3 (1988) 263–86.

———. "Suicide." In *The Anchor Yale Bible Dictionary*, edited by David Noel Freedman, 225–31. New York: Doubleday, 1992.

Droge, Arthur J., and James D. Tabor. *A Noble Death: Suicide and Martyrdom Among Christians and Jews in Antiquity*. San Francisco: HarperCollins, 1992.

Dublin, Louis I. "Suicide: A Sociological and Statistical Study." In *Comprehending Suicide: Landmarks in Twentieth-Century Suicidology*, edited by Edwin S. Shneidman, 49–58. Washington, DC: American Psychological Association, 2001.

Dunn, Geoffrey D. "Tertullian's Scriptural Exegesis in de Praescriptione Haereticorum." *Journal of Early Christian Studies* 14.2 (2006) 141–56.

Edelman, Diana Vilander. *King Saul in the Historiography of Judah*. Sheffield, UK: Sheffield, 1991.

Edwards, Mark J., ed. *Galatians, Ephesians, Philippians*. Downers Grove, IL: IVP Academic, 2005.

Ehrenberg, Victor, and A. H. M. Jones. *Documents Illustrating the Reigns of Augustus & Tiberius*. 2nd ed. Oxford: Clarendon, 1955.

Elliott, Neil, "The Apostle Paul and Empire." In *The Shadow of Empire: Reclaiming the Bible as a History of Faithful Resistance*, edited by Richard A. Horsley, 106. Louisville: Westminster John Knox, 2008.

Engberg-Pedersen, Troels. *Paul and the Stoics*. Louisville: Westminster John Knox, 2000.

———. "Stoicism in the Apostle Paul: A Philosophical Reading." In *Stoicism: Traditions and Transformations*, edited by Steven K. Strange and Jack Zupko, 52–74. Cambridge: Cambridge University Press, 2004.

Fagan, Garrett G. *The Lure of the Arena: Social Psychology and the Crowd at the Roman Games*. Cambridge/New York: Cambridge University Press, 2011.

Fairbairn, Gavin J., and Gavin Fairbairn. *Contemplating Suicide: The Language and Ethics of Self-Harm*. London/New York: Routledge, 1995.

Ferguson, Everett. *Backgrounds of Early Christianity*. 3rd ed. Grand Rapids, MI: Eerdmans, 2003.

Ferguson, John. *Pelagius: A Historical and Theological Study*. Cambridge: W. Heffer, 1956.

Finlan, Stephen. *The Background and Contents of Paul's Cultic Atonement Metaphors*. Leiden/Boston: Brill, 2004.

Finsterbusch, Karin, and Armin Lange. *Human Sacrifice in Jewish and Christian Tradition*. Leiden/Boston: Brill, 2006.

Fowler, W. Warde. *The Religious Experience of the Roman People*. Edinburgh: Echo Library, 2008.

Fox, Matthew. *The Reinvention of Work: New Vision of Livelihood for Our Time, A*. San Francisco: HarperOne, 1995.

Fredriksen, Paula. *Paul: The Pagans' Apostle*. New Haven: Yale University Press, 2017.

Frey, R. G. "Suicide and Self-Inflicted Death." *Philosophy* 56.216 (1981) 193–202.

Friesen, Steven, et al. *Corinth in Contrast: Studies in Inequality*. Lieden/Boston: Brill, 2013.

Fung, Ronald Y. K. *The Epistle to the Galatians*. 2nd rev. ed. Grand Rapids, MI: Eerdmans, 1988.

Futrell, Alison. *Blood in the Arena: The Spectacle of Roman Power*. Austin, TX: University of Texas Press, 2000.

———. *The Roman Games: A Sourcebook*. Malden, MA: Blackwell, 2006.

George, Timothy. *Galatians: An Exegetical and Theological Exposition of Holy Scripture*. Nashville, TN: Holman Reference, 1994.

Goldstein, Jonathan A. *II Maccabees*. Garden City, NY: Doubleday & Co., 1983.

Goodrich, John K. "Guardians, Not Taskmasters: The Cultural Resonances of Paul's Metaphor in Galatians 4.1–2." *Journal for the Study of the New Testament* 32.3 (2010) 251–84.

Guthrie, Tyson. "Irenaeus's Use of Galatians 4:4–5." Paper presented to the Society of Biblical Literature, November 2014. https://www.academia.edu/9583960/Irenaeuss_Use_of_Galatians_4_4–5.

Haig, Albert. "Neoplatonism as a Framework for Christian Theology: Reconsidering the Trinitarian Ontology of Marius Victorinus." *Pacifica* 21.2 (2008) 125–45.

Hardin, Justin K. *Galatians and the Imperial Cult: A Critical Analysis of the First-Century Social Context of Paul's Letter*. Tübingen: Mohr Siebeck, 2008.

Harnack, Adolf. *Der Kirchengeschichtliche Ertrag Der Exegistischen Arbeit Des Origens: II: Die Beiden Testament Mit Ausschluss Des Hexateuchs Und Des Richterbuchs*. Early Christian Literature. Reprint, Piscataway, NJ: Gorgias, 2010.

Hengel, Martin. *The Atonement: The Origins of the Doctrine in the New Testament*. Eugene, OR: Wipf & Stock, 2007.

———. *The Cross of the Son of God*. London: Hymns Ancient & Modern, 2012.

———. *Crucifixion*. Philadelphia: Fortress, 1977.

Hengel, Martin, and Roland Deines. *The Pre-Christian Paul*. London/Philadelphia: Trinity, 1991.

Hill, T. D. *Ambitiosa Mors: Suicide and the Self in Roman Thought and Literature*. New York: Routledge, 2004.

Holland, R. F. "Suicide." In *Against Empiricism*, by R. F. Holland, 143–57. Oxford: Blackwell, 1980.

Horsley, Richard A., ed. *In the Shadow of Empire: Reclaiming the Bible as a History of Faithful Resistance*. Louisville: Westminster John Knox, 2008.

Houtman, Alberdina, et al., eds. *The Actuality of Sacrifice: Past and Present*. Leiden/Boston: Brill, 2014.

Hunn, Debbie. "Christ versus the Law: Issues in Galatians 2:17–18." *Catholic Biblical Quarterly* 72.3 (2010) 537–55.

Hurtado, Larry W. *At the Origins of Christian Worship: The Context and Character of Earliest Christian Devotion*. Grand Rapids, MI: Eerdmans, 2000.

———. *How on Earth Did Jesus Become a God?: Historical Questions about Earliest Devotion to Jesus*. Grand Rapids, MI: Eerdmans, 2005.

———. *Lord Jesus Christ: Devotion to Jesus in Earliest Christianity*. Grand Rapids, MI: Eerdmans, 2005.

———. "Jesus as Lordly Example in Philippians 2:5–11." In *From Jesus to Paul: Studies in Honour of Francis Wright Beare*, edited by P. Richardson and J. C. Hurd, 113–26. Waterloo: Wilford Laurier University Press, 1984.

Inwagen, Peter van, and Dean Zimmerman, eds. *Persons: Human and Divine*. New York: Oxford University Press, 2007.

Jeffers, James S. *The Greco-Roman World of the New Testament Era: Exploring the Background of Early Christianity*. Downers Grove, IL: IVP Academic, 1999.

Johnson, Sherman E. "Early Christianity in Asia Minor." *Journal of Biblical Literature* 77.1 (1958) 39–58.

Kahl, Brigitte. *Galatians Re-Imagined: Reading With the Eyes of the Vanquished*. Minneapolis, MN: Fortress, 2010.

Koch, Dietrich-Alex. "Die Völkertafel von Josephus, Antiquitates Iudaicae I Und Das 'Galatien' Des Paulus." *Zeitschrift Für Die Neutestamentliche Wissenschaft Und Die Kunde Der Älteren Kirche* 103.1 (2012) 136–41.

Koch, H. J. "Suicides and Suicide Ideation in the Bible: An Empirical Survey." *Acta Psychiatrica Scandinavica* 112.3 (2005) 167–72.

Koester, Helmut. *Introduction to the New Testament*. Berlin: de Gruyter, 1995.

Krans, Jan, et al. *Paul, John, and Apocalyptic Eschatology: Studies in Honour of Martinus C. De Boer*. Leiden: Brill, 2013.

Kyle, Donald G. *Sport and Spectacle in the Ancient World*. 2 ed. West Sussex, UK: Wiley-Blackwell, 2014.

Larson, Edward J., and Darrel W. Amundsen. *A Different Death: Euthanasia & the Christian Tradition*. Downers Grove, IL: InterVarsity, 1998.

Lieu, Judith M. *Marcion and the Making of a Heretic: God and Scripture in the Second Century*. New York: Cambridge University Press, 2015.

Linebaugh, Jonathan A. *God, Grace, and Righteousness in Wisdom of Solomon and Paul's Letter to the Romans: Texts in Conversation*. Boston: Brill, 2013.

Longenecker, Richard N. *Galatians*. Grand Rapids, MI: Zondervan, 2015.

Lowery, Daniel DeWitt. "Oaths and Vows." In *Lexham Theological Wordbook*, edited by Douglas Mangum, et al. Lexham Bible Reference Series. Bellingham, WA: Lexham, 2014.

Lunn-Rockliffe, Sophie. *Ambrosiaster's Political Theology*. Oxford/New York: Oxford University Press, 2007.

Martyn, J. Louis. *Galatians*. New Haven: Yale University Press, 2004.

Matera, Frank J., and Daniel J. Harrington. *Galatians*. Collegeville, MN: Liturgical, 2007.

McGowan, Andrew. "God in Christ." In *Tertullian and Paul*, edited by Todd D. Still and David Wilhite, 1–15. New York: T. & T. Clark, 2013.

McKnight, Scot, and Joseph B. Modica, eds. *Jesus Is Lord, Caesar Is Not: Evaluating Empire in New Testament Studies*. Downers Grove, IL: IVP Academic, 2013.

Middleton, Paul. "Early Christian Voluntary Martyrdom: A Statement for the Defence." *J Theol Studies* 64.2 (2013) 556–73.

———. *Radical Martyrdom and Cosmic Conflict in Early Christianity*. London/New York: T. & T. Clark, 2006.

Miles, Jack. *Christ: A Crisis in the Life of God*. New York: Vintage, 2002.

Mitchell, Stephen. *The Celts in Anatolia and the Impact of Roman Rule*. Vol. 1 of *Anatolia: Land, Men, and Gods in Asia Minor*. Rev. ed. Oxford: Clarendon, 1995.

Moo, Douglas J., et al. *Galatians*. Grand Rapids, MI: Baker Academic, 2013.

Morris, Leon. *Apostolic Preaching of the Cross. Revised.* 3rd ed. Grand Rapids, MI Eerdmans, 1965.

Moss, Candida. *The Myth of Persecution: How Early Christians Invented a Story of Martyrdom.* New York: Harper Collins, 2013.

Neufeld, Dietmar. "Social Sciences and the New Testament." *Oxford Bibliographies,* September 13, 2010. http://www.oxfordbibliographies.com/view/document/obo-9780195393361/obo-9780195393361-0117.xml.

Neusner, Jacob. "Genesis Rabbah as Polemic: An Introductory Account." *Hebrew Annual Review* 9 (1985) 253–65.

Nickelsburg, George W. E. *Resurrection, Immortality, and Eternal Life in Intertestamental Judaism and Early Christianity.* Expanded ed. Cambridge, MA: Harvard Divinity School, 2007.

Novenson, Matthew V. *Christ among the Messiahs: Christ Language in Paul and Messiah Language in Ancient Judaism.* New York: Oxford University Press, 2012.

O'Brien, Peter T. *The Epistle to the Philippians.* Grand Rapids, MI: Eerdmans, 1991.

O'Connell, John P. *The Eschatology of Saint Jerome.* Mundelein, IL: Apud aedes Seminarii Sanctae Mariae ad Lacum, 1948.

Pfitzner, V. C. *Paul and the Agon Motif: Traditional Athletic Imagery in the Pauline Literature.* Leiden: Brill, 1967.

Plumer, Eric. *Augustine's Commentary on Galatians: Introduction, Text, Translation, and Notes.* Oxford/New York: Oxford University Press, 2006.

Porter, Stanley E. *Paul and His Social Relations.* Leiden/Boston: Brill, 2012.

Pöschl, Viktor. *The Art of Vergil: Image and Symbol in the Aeneid.* Ann Arbor: University of Michigan Press, 1962.

Ramsay, W. M. "Studies in the Roman Province Galatia: I. The Homanadeis and the Homanadensian War." *The Journal of Roman Studies* 7 (1917) 229–83.

Rawson, Elizabeth. "Religion and Politics in the Late Second Century BC at Rome." *Phoenix* 28.2 (1974) 193–212.

Reumann, John. *Philippians: A New Translation with Introduction and Commentary.* Anchor Yale Bible 33B. New Haven: Yale University Press, 2008.

Riches, John. *Galatians Through the Centuries.* Oxford: Wiley-Blackwell, 2013.

Rosner, Fred. "Suicide in Biblical, Talmudic, and Rabbinic Writings." *Tradition* 11.2 (1970) 25–40.

Scheck, Thomas P., trans. *St. Jerome's Commentaries on Galatians, Titus, and Philemon.* Notre Dame: University of Notre Dame Press, 2010.

Schilling, Robert. "Roman Religion." In *Historia Religionum,* edited by C. J. Bleeker and G. Widengren, 474. Leiden: Brill, 1969.

Schmid, Ulrich. *Marcion und sein Apostolos.* Berlin/New York: De Gruyter, 1995.

Schneemelcher, Wilhelm, and Robert McLachlan Wilson. *New Testament Apocrypha: Writings Relating to the Apostles, Apocalypses, and Related Subjects.* Louisville: Westminster John Knox, 2003.

Schnelle, Udo. *Apostle Paul: His Life and Theology.* Grand Rapids, MI: Baker Academic, 2005.

———. *Theology of the New Testament.* Translated by M. Eugene Boring and M. Boring. Grand Rapids, MI: Baker Academic, 2009.

Schwally, Friedrich. *Das Leben Nach Dem Tode.* BiblioBazaar, 2009.

Schwartz, Daniel R. *2 Maccabees.* Berlin/New York: de Gruyter, 2008.

Schweizer, Eduard. *Erniedrigung Und Erhöhung Bei Jesus Und Seinen Nachfolgern.* Zurich: Zwingli-Verlag, 1962.

Searle, John R. *Intentionality: An Essay in the Philosophy of Mind.* Cambridge/New York: Cambridge University Press, 1983.

Seo, J. Mira. *Exemplary Traits: Reading Characterization in Roman Poetry.* Oxford: Oxford University Press, 2013.

Sevenster, Jan Nicolaas. *Paul and Seneca.* Leiden: Brill, 1961.

Snyder, Graydon F. *Irish Jesus, Roman Jesus: The Formation of Early Irish Christianity.* Harrisburg, PA: Trinity, 2002.

Sorabji, Richard. *The Philosophy of the Commentators, 200–600 AD, A Sourcebook: Logic and Metaphysics.* Ithaca, NY: Cornell University Press, 2005.

Souter, Alexander. *Earliest Latin Commentaries On the Epistles of St. Paul.* Oxford: Oxford University Press, 1999.

———. *A Study of Ambrosiaster.* Reprint, Oxford: Nabu, 2014.

Stevens, Susan T. "A Legend of the Destruction of Carthage." *Classical Philology* 83.1 (1988) 39–41.

Still, Todd D., and David Wilhite, eds. *Tertullian and Paul.* New York: T. & T. Clark, 2013.

Thompson, R. J. *Penitence and Sacrifice in Early Israel Outside the Levitical Law: Examination of the Fellowship Theory of Early Israelite Sacrifice.* Leiden: Brill, n.d.

Tolmie, D. Francois. *Persuading the Galatians: A Text-Centred Rhetorical Analysis of a Pauline Letter.* Tübingen: Mohr Siebeck, 2005.

Tov, Emanuel. "Textual History of the Song of Deborah in the a Text of the LXX." *Vetus Testamentum* 28.2 (1978) 224–32.

Vermeulen, Frank, et al. "The Imperial Sanctuary at Pessinus and Its Predecessors: A Revision." *Anata* 3.1 (1995) 125–44.

Versnel, H. S. "Self-Sacrifice, Compensation, and the Anonymous Gods." In *Le Sacrifice dans l'Antiquité,* edited by Jean Rudhardt and Olivier Reverdin, 135–85. Entretiens sur l'Antiquité Classique 27. Vandœuvres–Genève: Fondations Hardt, 1980.

———. "Two Types of Roman Devotio." *Mnemosyne* 29.4 (1976) 365–410.

Watt, JG van der, ed. *Salvation in the New Testament: Perspectives on Soteriology.* Atlanta, GA: SBL, 2004.

Weinreich, Otto. *Antike Heilungswunder: Untersuchungen Zum Wunderglauben Der Griechen Und Römer.* Berlin: de Gruyter, 1969.

Wenham, Gordon J. *Numbers.* Downers Grove, IL: IVP Academic, 2008.

Wenkel, David H., and John B. Song. "The Image of God and the Cosmos: A Response to the Individualist Critique of Penal Substitutionary Atonement." *Reformed Theological Review* 71.1 (2012) 1–20.

White, Hayden. *Tropics of Discourse: Essays in Cultural Criticism.* Reprint, Baltimore, MD: Johns Hopkins University Press, 1986.

Wiedemann, Thomas. *Emperors and Gladiators.* Rev. ed. London/New York: Routledge, 1995.

Wiles, Maurice F. *The Divine Apostle: The Interpretation of St. Paul's Epistles in the Early Church.* Cambridge: Cambridge University Press, 1967.

Williams, Jarvis J. *Maccabean Martyr Traditions in Pauls Theology of Atonement: Did Martyr Theology Shape Pauls Conception of Jesus Death?* Eugene, OR: Wipf & Stock, 2010.

Williams, Sam K. *Jesus' Death As Saving Event the Background and Origin of a Concept.* Missoula, MT: Scholars, 1975.

Wright, N. T. *The Climax of the Covenant: Christ and the Law in Pauline Theology.* Minneapolis: Fortress, 1991.

———. *Paul and the Faithfulness of God.* Minneapolis: Fortress, 2013.

Yerkes, Royden Keith, and Joachim Wach. *Sacrifice in Greek and Roman Religions and Early Judaism:* Reprint, Eugene, OR: Wipf & Stock, 2010.

Printed in Dunstable, United Kingdom

70265779R00094